MW00776458

HALLWAY LEADERSHIP

Being a Leader who is Present and
Visible inside the hallways of your school.

Derrick Sier
Katie Kinder
Taylor Upchurch

DEDICATION

Dedicated to all our children. The ones we raise and the ones we educate. You are loved. Go change the world!

NEMLC

Copyright 2023 The Blue Wall LLC.

Print ISBN: 978-1-66789-586-4

eBook ISBN: 978-1-66789-587-1

Within these pages lies opinions, suggestions, stories, and advice of educators, community leaders, and world changers with over 200 years of combined experience in the field of education. You will learn, grow, laugh, and cry. Come in learners; we are going on a journey together!

We would like to thank our contributing authors for making this project possible. May we change the world one school at a time!

(Listed in Alphabetical Order)

Marcus Belin	**Shay Omokhomion**	**Charles Williams**
Heady Coleman	**Erin Patton**	**Tron Young**
Shari Gateley	**Andrea Sifers**	
Cindi Hemm	**Adam Welcome**	

ABOUT THE AUTHORS:

Derrick Sier is an acclaimed facilitator, author of My Life of Lists, Small Stories, Big Team, and Dear Ricky. Over the last 20 years, Derrick's passion for social and group dynamics has reached every area of his life. Using his B.S. in Kinesiology, M.A. in Theological Studies, 20+ years of community and culture experience in the education and corporate settings. Derrick shares his love for people and the betterment of the environments in which they connect around the world. He is a dad, a husband, and a fierce friend.

Katie Kinder, author of *Untold Teaching Truths,* is a professional learning facilitator, and she has been an educator since 2006. She brings her message of hope, fun, and real strategies to educators all over the nation. She believes that life is fun, and learning should most definitely be fun. A teacher of the year, top five district finalist, Speaker, Author, Professional Development Leader, a Mom, a Wife, a Fierce Advocate for Education, OKC Rotary Teacher of the Month, and grant award winner, Katie has learned a trick or two in the classroom, so come on in, and have some fun, and hook your students from day one!

Taylor Upchurch is a seasoned educator with over 18 years of experience in the field. He holds a B.S. in Secondary Education and a M.A. in Educational Leadership. He is a proud father and husband and values his family as his top priority. Taylor lives by his personal motto of "be patient and show grace." He is a natural leader and communicator, and has a talent for bringing people together and fostering a sense of community. Taylor has led numerous professional development sessions on classroom management and building positive relationships within the classroom.

CONTENTS

CHAPTER ONE:

The People's Principal

Katie Kinder

"A positive culture beats strategy any day of the week."

I worked for a man named John for years. He is the principal I want all teachers to have at some point in their careers. When I worked for him, he redeemed my hope in the education system, in society, in people, in life.

He was skinny, lanky even. Goofy. He loved to laugh and joke around, and he genuinely cared about people. We were always people first in John's eyes. Before we were a warm body in a classroom, a piece of data, a lesson plan, a teacher, we were valued as human beings.

I was coming off a few years at a toxic school. If you do this long enough, you will work in a positive culture, and unfortunately in a toxic one. It is one of the inevitable pitfalls in a broken education sphere. If you are reading this and you've never worked in a school that felt toxic, please reach out because I want to interview you!

I was gun shy when I came to John decently early in my career. I came to his school from a place of trauma. I was at a point in my teaching career that I did not know if I wanted to continue this journey. We all have these thoughts as educators. I entered this new school year with not only my heart broken a little, but my body was broken too. Four days before school started, I tore my entire left knee out playing soccer on a turf indoor field. It was the triple tear of terrible. I got my ACL, my MCL, and my meniscus all in one fell swoop. I wish I could tell you it was because I was doing something amazingly cool, diving header over four players to score the winning goal. Nope. I was all alone and twisted wrong. Pop. Pop. Pop. went my left knee.

So there I was. Broken heart. Broken body. Crutches and sadness. I had to wear a backpack and crutch down to make copies, and crutch back. I crutched around my classroom and every once in a while I would teach on a stool with my whole leg elevated to keep the swelling at bay. I would teach all day to the best of my ability, cry in the car all the way to physical therapy, cry the whole time at physical therapy, cry the whole way home, and finally pull it together for my family to make dinner and prepare my mind to do it all again the next day. My kids were toddlers at the time, and I had to be strong for them.

For the next year, I was quiet. If you know me at all, to say the adjective 'quiet' is laughable. I am not. But this particular year, I was. I observed. I learned, and watched, and grew as a leader. The first month, I rested in the fact that this school was NOT toxic, not even close, not even a little bit. The levity I felt in my soul was something I cannot describe to you. John observed my teaching on a near daily basis; he is relational. He started to see that even on one leg, I was pretty dang good. He immediately put me on the principal's leadership team, the guiding coalition, and made me a team leader. "Oh," I thought to myself, "Maybe I am meant for this career." He poured into me as an educator, so I could pour into my students as a teacher. This was heart and soul work, and John was the heartbeat of our building.

John was the epitome of a hallway leader. If you needed John, he was not far away. He wholeheartedly believed that if students were in the school, he would not be doing any sort of paperwork. He never hid in his office; he was there. It made the school feel safe like a family.

John did lunch duty every single day. He was never not there. For three hours of every single school day, Monday through Friday, he monitored, led, herded, laughed with, and disciplined the 600 students in and out of the lunch room. I often only guessed at his exhaustion while the teachers in his school were blessed with this glorious, thirty minutes of lunch bliss.

Sometimes, in a school full of middle school kids, with hormones raging, and power dynamics in the balance, drama will ensue; that is the nature of teaching in middle school. In unstructured environments, some kids will take advantage of the walk from lunch back to the classroom. (Only some). See, I work in a school in which, statistically, it is the third most violent neighborhood in our urban city. They won't deliver pizzas to the housing projects I am referring to; that is my student population. Now, don't get it twisted, my students are smart, capable, beautiful, and often exist within a cycle of poverty in which the only way out is their education. But, if pride is the only thing that belongs to you, you will physically fight for that pride. And, that happens, often.

On this particular day, John was leading the herd down the hallway back to their 8th grade classes to close out the afternoon as he did every school day. Then it happened, we saw it happening as if in slow motion. I'm standing at my door, crutches in hand when two girls drop their backpacks, the kids circle up, phones come out, cameras come on, and these two girls start wailing on each other. Both girls were in my class in different hours. It was February, so there should be no doubt in your mind that as their teacher, I loved each one of them as I had poured into them since August, and wanted to see their success.

It was the most violent fight I had ever witnessed in my years as an educator, and that is saying a lot. I had witnessed my fair share of horrific fights since 2006. In a whirl of blood, hair, broken noses, screams, and utter sadness, we broke it up. John, Coach Jones, and myself were able to push through and physically restrain these precious babies who thought the only avenue to resolution was to take the other one out. Arrests were made, and we got our kids back in class, and I looked out into the hall with pencils, backpacks, phones, blood, hair strewn all over, I thought to myself, "this can't be here when the bell rings for 6th hour." I was on my hands and knees cleaning before I even realized what I was doing; bloodborne pathogens be damned. Tears streaming down my face, I'm placing things in a trash bag when I look up. On his hands and knees, tears streaming down his face, bloodborne pathogens be damned, was John. The Hallway Leader I hope you all have one day. The servant leader I pray every teacher on this planet will have one day.

-Katie Kinder

CHAPTER TWO:

Out of Sight, Out of Mind

Derrick Sier

There is something wonderfully powerful about being seen in a school hallway. Just simply being in the eye-shot of the students does something magical to the atmosphere. Their behavior changes. Their speech changes. Their volume changes. Seriously, as a teacher, administrator, heck, even as a plain-ole adult, just your presence has power. I'm not even talking about saying anything, interacting with anyone or even moving throughout the hallway space to strategically position yourself amongst students. I'm simply talking about how your presence has an influence and it moves the environment by standing in one place and being visible. It shifts behavior and raises the awareness when students know someone is there and they are watching.

Let's take it outside of the school and into real-life adulthood situations. I drive differently when law enforcement is around. It's funny and it's true. The content of my jokes and color of my language changes when children and students are in ear-shot. When important people are in the room, my attention is redirected to them. When I'm with a client, my focus narrows and there is an exerted attempt to be more articulate and concise in my explanations. When me and the fellas are hanging out and my wife walks into the room, our humor changes. When my mom is around, even as an adult, the level of my manners and respect increases. Presence matters! People intentionally adjust when they know others are watching. When we are aware that a certain standard of behavior is expected and the carriers or enforcers of that behavior are in the place, we know how to navigate the space.

So, why does watching matter? First, you can learn a lot about a student based on what they say, but you can also learn just as much, if not more, by watching what they do. Let's consider social dynamics. By simply watching, you can identify who is popular, who is the bully, who is the target of bullying, who belongs to which clique, which student is selling candy or anything else, who is dating and how everyone feels about it. By watching, you get to see drama unfold and prevent it from happening. By watching, you get to identify the potential hotspots in the hallway and school for mischief. By watching, you get to notice body language and other responses to environmental stimuli. And don't think the students aren't watching you as well. They are forming and shaping their individual and collective perspective of you by how you behave, interact, respond, position and all the other things as well.

Secondly, watching matters because the hallway overflows into the classroom. The hallway can provide additional information and context to academic performance and low or hyper-social involvement. You can call them clues, indicators, causality, correlation...whatever language you want to use, USE IT. Just know, while the physical spaces are separate, they definitely impact each other. The hallway is one space. The classroom is another. The student is in both. And because the student is impacted by both environments of the school, teachers and administrators must be aware of what's happening in both areas as well. It doesn't even require an extensive investigative approach. It simply requires… you guessed it… your presence.

Lastly, being present and watching matters because being out of sight can often equate to being out of mind. As education professionals, we sign up to make our students our focus. How does that happen? For most education professions, it is less about WHAT we are teaching and mostly about

WHO we are teaching. And if we only get these young people for six to eight hours a day, we should want to make the most of it. This means, we want to be present, active and impactful on as many levels and in as many areas as possible. Playgrounds. Lunch rooms. Classrooms. Hallways. Parking lots. Sports stadiums. Student led clubs. The hallway doesn't just connect classroom to classroom, the hallway should connect the educational professional to the heart and life of their student. We don't get that access by sitting at our desk during passing periods. We don't get that connection by hiding during down time. We don't develop that trust by turning a blind eye. We don't get to have that impact and influence by only being visible inside the four walls of the classroom. We get that magic, the ability, and power to shift environments and the correlating behavior simply by being present in the hallways of the school and in the hallways of the heart.

Step out. Be present. Stretch those legs. Open your eyes. Tune up your spidey senses. Seek to become more involved. And take pride in manning your post… in the hallway.

-Derrick Sier

CHAPTER THREE:

Following the Lead, The AP

Taylor Upchurch

The role of the assistant principal encompasses many things, but the most important thing is to follow the lead of the head principal. "Periodt," as our students might say. Full stop. No questions. The assistant principal is ultimately an extension of the building leader. The assistant principal's primary focus is to be a supportive leader, and we should work in tandem with the head principal to ensure the school's mission and vision is accomplished. I'd even go as far as to say that if you're not on board with what the head principal is doing, then you need to go elsewhere. This relationship cannot be competitive. You are not trying to run your own school or one-up the head principal. This teamwork and understanding is crucial to the success of the school. I've been lucky to be in places where this team mentality is being practiced, but I have colleagues that have had different experiences. You may also know someone in a similar school where competition among leaders eventually drains the energy from the building. This behavior is detrimental to the culture of the school. Your teachers feel this and in the end the students suffer.

I've heard on multiple occasions that the assistant principal should have a goal of one day becoming a lead principal. I've had mentors tell me that in an encouraging way, and I've also heard it said in a condescending way. As in, "if you don't want to be a head principal one day, why would you want to be an assistant?" I've been told that if you're not wanting and willing to become a head principal, then your mindset is not in the right place. I've also witnessed many assistant principals that are great in the position and have no desire to lead their own building. I don't think there is a right or wrong way to approach the question, but I do believe that the assistant principal must often think like a head principal. They are not mere disciplinarians and will eventually need to make important decisions for the school.

I once attended a professional development on restorative discipline and it was said that assistant principals are water movers. A student messes up. The AP removes the student for a number of days. The kid reenters the classroom and oftentimes has the same behavior. The presenter joked that an assistant principal, who is reduced to just a disciplinarian, can't make water into wine. This cycle is a huge misuse of the assistant principal. I would suggest that schools instead utilize the APs to be in classrooms more often and work with the teachers on how to correct unwanted behaviors. Some of the biggest leaps I ever had as a teacher were because my evaluating assistant principal had conversations with me. Mrs. Land was a career AP. She had been at the same school for 15+ years and she was great at her job. Honestly, I didn't realize this until five or six years into my career. At first I thought Mrs. Land was just giving me extra tasks to complete. Why wouldn't she just let me teach? It wasn't until later in my career that I realized her job was to make me a better teacher. The one thing that she pushed me to do was to reflect. Reflect on a daily lesson, reflect on how I interacted with a certain kid. I hated hearing that word sometimes because it made me see what I needed to change. Reflect. Sometimes as teachers we work at such a quick pace and move quickly to the next lesson. We've got papers to grade and labs to set up. I was very bad, and still am, about stopping and reflecting. I'm working on it; it is something I still have to remind myself to do daily or at the end of each week. I wish Mrs. Land was around to remind me to slow down and reflect.

Our role as the assistant principal is critical to the success of a school, but it should always be in alignment with the vision and mission of the head principal. Assistant principals can be effective leaders in their own right by working closely with teachers to improve student behavior and performance. As demonstrated by the example of Mrs. Land, reflecting on one's teaching practices can be a powerful tool for professional growth, and assistant principals can play a crucial role in facilitating this process. Ultimately, a successful school requires a team effort and a shared commitment to student success.

-Taylor Upchurch

CHAPTER FOUR:

"So you want to be a Public School Principal?"

Advice to the newly appointed from a veteran who has #beenthere
Cindi Hemm

Well, Let me start out by introducing myself. I have been in education since 1979 and have seen the pendulum of education swing through many trends. I was a speech pathologist from 1979-1994 and an elementary principal from 1995-2012. I retired, but I could not stay away; I went back to work as a rural superintendent/principal from 2016-2020. I loved every stage of my career with my whole heart.

I have been asked to give advice to those "novice building administrators" aka – "baby principals." Here is my first tip: "It is lonely at the top." You have probably just left a building where you were a teacher. You never lacked for friends; you may have been the teacher of the year, and your community was always within your reach because you loved your school and there was always a teacher to befriend. You had many wonderful times;

dare I say, even some pretty fun happy hours after the days in the trenches with your best teacher friends alongside you.

However, The announcement has just been made that you are the new principal of a new school and you enter a building where you are in charge. BEWARE – you officially now have zero friends in your current assignment. You are their boss and many will pretend that they like or respect you, but make no mistake; respect is earned. Watch what you say and what you do from the moment the announcement is made naming you as the new leader. Clean up your social media and delete any pics that any parent or boss will find offensive and as time goes by, you will find out who you can trust and who you cannot. Keep your own counsel and if you need to have a sounding board that understands what you are going through, call a fellow principal, preferably one with at least four years experience, and ask their opinion or just vent. Every baby principal needs a principal mentor in another building. Think of your teachers as you would think of your class; you love them; you serve them; you make sure they are cared for, but you are not their friend!

Do you feel as though you are drowning, or bobbing up for air every once in a while. Are you gasping for air or do you often think to yourself, "when will I swim?" I have always said your first year you drown in reports, teacher issues, student issues, education service center issues and always, parent issues. Your second year, you can bob up for air, and yet still it can feel like an impossible job. However, in your second year, if you've done your job, you know your staff. You realize whom you can trust and whom you cannot. The workload is the same, but somehow you are better prepared and know what will be coming down that principal pipe. This is the year you can move teachers into different positions, or sometimes, a necessary part of your job will be identifying those staff members who do not belong in your building. Do it with kindness, but be clear with them, and advise them to teach elsewhere or if they are detrimental to children, let them know they should pick a different career path entirely.

Your third year is when you are swimming. Sometimes with sharks i.e. students, parents, and teachers, but swimming nonetheless, and doing what is best for the students. In every decision, every decision, in every move that you make as the principal in your building, do what is right for kids. When you lead in this manner, and make all decisions based on what is best for the students, you will succeed, and the teachers who are willing to follow your lead, will stay. The others won't, and that is okay. Sometimes the decisions you make will not be what is best for teachers and their comfort, and you have to be tough enough to handle it.

Put on your armor each day because teachers will talk about you just as we did as teachers, and I prefer that. Talk behind my back. Our job is too big, too life changing to be listening to idle gossip. Also, those carrying tales to you, are not your friend; they are probably the pot stirrers. If I had teachers constantly trying to encourage a toxic culture, I attempted to get rid of those people. At times, I could even convince them they would be much happier in another building. Our kids are watching; how do we speak about one another, how do we treat one another? When you throw yourself into your building 110% of the time, you are doing the best job you know how to do. However, if a staff member is complaining about a problem, give me a solution. I was not naive enough to believe we wouldn't have problems. As a principal, you should rely on your best teachers, your innovators, and empower them to find solutions to problems. As the head principal, you will make hundreds of decisions each and every day. Many will have to be instantaneous: the toilet is overflowing in the bathroom, there is a fight in the boys' bathroom, you hear shots fired when you are on the playground with kids, a teacher's husband has been in an accident and she needs to leave now, a four year old is yelling the "F-word" at breakfast, a teacher just flipped off another teacher in the hall and kids saw it, a teacher showed up drunk to teach his class, a parent is yelling at another parent in the hall, a gang member snuck into the school and is walking down the hall threatening his brother's tormentors, the superintendent makes a surprise visit, you have an outbreak of a contagion, you have five teachers out sick with no subs, your electricity stopped working at 9:00 a.m. now what? All of those things happened to me. So, idle gossip, no. You will have those staff members that feel it is their job to tell on other staff members, and you must stop that ASAP or they will come to you every day. Rely on your innovators, your best teachers to find solutions to problems while you grab the plunger and run into the bathroom for the third time that day!

Oh the tears, the many tears. You will shed many tears in this position, but you learn from each and every mistake. I never wanted to think I knew it all; mistakes are made and growth must happen. I loved my staff, students, and parents. I went to their weddings and their family funerals. I have attended many students' funeral services as well. There is nothing sadder nor nothing that needs your support more than a family that has had a sudden loss. You must be there. This job will also shatter your heart, but you must be there.

I lived by the mantra, people-work during the day, and paperwork at night or on the weekends. If kids are in the building, you are in classrooms, the hallways, the lunch room, the playground. Only when students leave, does the paperwork begin. I often worked twelve hour days, and another eight hours on Sundays after church just as your teachers do with planning, grading, and growing. Lead by example. During a school day, my door was open not that you could find me there, but I was often called in to deal with an angry parent, or someone who needed a shoulder to cry on. I prayed with staff members and parents who were going through tremendous loss. Here is a great tip: find a secret place in the building, just once a week for an uninterrupted hour and organize. I would go into the Library closet and sit on the floor and get my "to do" list in order, going through all the scraps of paper with important notes and phone numbers and got organized. The only person who knew my location was my administrative assistant. I would tell her, " if the building is burning, come get me, or my bosses show up unexpectedly, come get me!" Then, she was sworn to secrecy of my location.

Do hard things; Don't put them off. Get these off your plate imme-diately. Call the irate parent, go sit in the classroom of the teacher and do their evaluation even if you know it is not going to go well, write the "plan of improvement" for a staff member, and do that with kindness after school on a Friday, so they can get their bearings by Monday. Surround yourself with competent and trustworthy leadership in your building. When I chose my team leaders, I made sure they were good teachers with good relationships with their peers. We could talk about some tough decisions that had to be made and they made me see situations in a different light.

The culture of the building goes by way of the leader. You must lead in a positive, forward thinking manner. I always said, "I am driving the bus. You may dance on the bus and even change seats, but make no mistake, if you try to get off my bus, I will help you leave my bus." I told each and every child every day that I loved them, and it was so wonderful to see their faces. Every day. Each child and adult in your building needs to feel welcome and loved, especially those kids that are so hard to love. Buffer your teachers, protect them. Do not ever, ever allow your staff to be belittled or verbally abused by anyone. You are getting paid "the big bucks." It is your job to protect your staff from verbal abuse; get between the irate parent and the teacher. Tell that parent to come to your office so you can hear their complaint. If they will not cooperate, escort them off the premises. If they will not leave, call the police. Parents usually just want to be heard. Parents who exist inside a cycle of poverty will "perform" in front of their kids to show them how much they love them. That is a crazy, but based in education research, fact. 99% of the time when you get them in your office, they will calm down. Do not meet with an angry parent with the child present. Separate them. Tell the student that the adults must talk, and then bring the child in. This will give time for the parent to calm down and discuss the problem reasonably. Cameras have been a great asset for the principal. It is hard to deny the visual from the camera when the child has told the parent a completely different story. Rely on the story the camera tells. You may completely agree with what the parent has told you, but never undermine a teacher in front of a parent. I would say, "I would be upset too if my own child came home and told me that. Let me speak to the teacher and get the adult version." Always buffer for your teachers.

Install a sensory room in your school immediately. I wish I had known about this concept my first few years of being an elementary principal as it would have made life so much easier. Many of our students need an outlet to work off some energy, a safe, calm down place. This room is typically manned by a teacher assistant or paraprofessional. Make sure your sensory room has indirect or natural light. Instrumental music, couches, soft chairs, weighted blankets, stationary bikes, and a stairmaster. We had a few desks as well as a few yoga mats. This is an area for students that are having a tough time focusing and need a break. We called it a "time in" room not a "time out" room. They can stay for fifteen to twenty minutes. The para can see if the child wants to do yoga, ride the bike, or simply do some breathing exercises on the couch. Soon the student is calm enough to return to class. You have to have the right person to be in charge and they must buy into this type of cool down method. This practice cut our office referrals in half the first year it was in place, and by three fourths the second year. Every school needs this type of room.

You are charged with leading the best school in the whole wide world! You should say it every day, and by your third year, it should be true! The more you say it, believe it, and know it, the more the students, parents, teachers, and community will say it, believe it, and know it to be absolutely true.

You are in the very best job to affect positive change within an entire community. Lead with kindness, lead with positivity. Tell your staff, "Do not mistake my kindness for weakness!" It actually takes a strong personality to infuse kindness with firmness. Be tough. Good Luck on this venture, new principal; it isn't for everyone, but when done well, it is a glorious feeling to look back and be proud of a job well done!

-Cindi Hemm

Cindi Hemm, author of Miracle on Southwest Boulevard, is a teacher, principal, and superintendent; She has a masters degree from Northeastern University. She has been an educator since 1979. She has won Tulsa Public School's Principal of the year, twice, once in 2008 and again in 2010. She won the prestigious Oklahoma Foundation of Excellence award in 2011. A speaker, an author, an award winner, a staunch advocate for children and public schools, Cindi is now retired and lives in Broken Arrow with her husband and spends her days with her family and thirteen grandchildren.

CHAPTER FIVE:

The Servant Leader

Katie Kinder

"Leadership without servanthood is simply manipulation."
-Jerrod Murr

It is 2006, and I was pregnant with my first baby. My pregnancy was wrought with complications. My husband and I had a hard time trying to get pregnant and after four years of marriage, we turned to fertility treatments. Alas, it worked. I was pregnant with twins. When I was eight weeks pregnant, my fallopian tube ruptured because another baby was trapped there and no one knew. I was rushed to the hospital the day before school started. The. Day. Before. Any teacher or principal reading this knows the hectic nature of the day right before school starts and kids flood the front doors. There are copies to be made, decorations to hang, lessons to plan, seating charts to make, class schedules in a constant state of updating, desks to find, and the list goes on.

I was rushed into emergency surgery with hushed prayers on my lips that my babies would be okay. My husband was there in a blur, and although my parents lived two hours away, they were there too, but as I waited alone for my family to arrive, it was the administrators from my school who sat with me and held my hand. They had a thousand other things they needed to get done before kids came, but there they were. I was in and out of consciousness as I bled out internally. Looking back on it now, I know I almost lost my life that day, but at the time, I didn't understand the gravity of the situation.

I came to after surgery to have the doctor come in and explain what happened.

"You were pregnant with twins," she said, "But what we didn't know was that there was a third fetus in your tube, and as the fetus grew, it ruptured your fallopian tube. Fetus B and Fetus C are gone." We stared at her in disbelief.

"Okay," I answered groggily, "What about my baby A."

She answered me, "Fetus A will miscarry; it is only a matter of time. I'm sorry."

"BABY A is going to live," I said to her as she walked out of the door and my husband gathered me up in the hospital bed ever so gingerly. We cried. We sobbed. I tearily promised him, "Baby A is going to live."

Each week of my pregnancy after that, my OBGYN promised me the baby would miscarry, but it didn't happen. "My miracle baby," I would whisper to my belly, "meant to walk the earth."

Ten weeks after my life-saving emergency surgery, I was allowed to go back to school. I was teaching high school English. Each step I took hurt, each day my belly grew, I hurt. My school at the time wrapped me up in care. The assistant principal gave me his parking spot directly next to the school, so I wouldn't have to walk from the teacher's parking lot forever away. Thanks, Tim. I was working in one of the largest high schools in the state, so the staff was largely broken up by department. One could work there several years and not know every staff member.

The English department became my family. Coach Wright down the hall checked on me almost every day, and carried things for me if needed. I was given directives by the doctor to not lift anything more than five pounds. Thanks, Eddie!

All the principals at the building moved my classroom downstairs close to the exit, and the teacher's room I took gladly gave up her room to make sure I was safe. They moved my whole room and organized it. The principals.

Our head principal, Sam, was a funny guy. He loved the kids and teachers; he was meant to be in the field of education. He was always coming up with new, fun ways to build community for everyone who walked his halls. He interacted with parents, kids, teachers, and staff each day. When you were in the presence of Sam, you felt lighthearted and like you were his favorite person on earth. Full attentiveness, kindness, and inside jokes abounded in his school. His Family School. There were five assistant principals under him, and he could have very much sat back and been a figurehead while his APs did the brunt of the work, but no. You could find him picking up chairs, cleaning spills in the cafeteria, wearing mascot costumes through the halls, being present, and walking the building each day. He truly had his thumb on the pulse of the school. And our school community culture was better for it.

I was eight months pregnant in February 2007. There I was teaching my pregnant heart out. I had gotten so big that I could not see my own feet, and my feet would sweat so profusely that I wore flip flops every day, and I only half hoped they were a matching pair. We were having a little girl. Miracle Baby Girl.

I still taught the way I knew I should for the ninth grade babies in my English class. I was on my swollen, sweaty feet all day. I remember my belly being so big that I tried to walk the rows to help kids with their essay writing and when I turned around my belly smacked a kid in the face.

"Ms. Kinder!" my mortified student whispered, "Your belly just hit me in the face!" We laughed so hard that day, and then in walked Sam. The head principal.

"Katie," he said, "Can I talk with you?" No matter what kind of teacher you are, if you are the teacher of the year four years in a row, when the principal says he needs to talk to you, your stomach drops out. The kids were all, "Ooooooooooo, Ms. Kinder is in trouble!"

He said, "Have you looked outside?"

"No," I answered.

"It is icing and snowing and it is going to get bad. I will be taking over your classes for the rest of the day while you get home. Please let me know when you've made it home safely. Be well."

I was in my twenties at the time and this was the only school I had ever worked at, so I didn't know how rare and wonderful this moment was until later in my career when I worked for other principals who were the antithesis of Sam. I grabbed my purse, coat, and stopped short of grabbing the stacks of papers that needed to be graded because Sam wouldn't let me. I left with "Bye Ms. Kinder; we love you," ringing in my ears as I eased out of the parking spot that was given to me, so I would be safe.

We were out of school for a whole week after that snowmageddon, and I found out later that we had three other teachers at the time who were pregnant, and they were sent home early as the APs covered their classes too. When a snow like that happens in Oklahoma, the kids start to get checked out early, the buses come early, and the very small portion of kids left at the end of the day were in the gym with the principals because our admin team sent each and every teacher home early in hopes they were safe too.

This is servant leadership, and with a servant's heart, Sam stayed at his school for many years before he became a superintendent at a small district, and guess what? He did the same thing there. Thanks, Sam. You are forever a gem in my journey as an educator, and every principal I've ever had after has been compared to you and your heart to serve people. My Miracle Maddy was born on March 13th, 2007. Baby A lives! She does live with some challenges, but she defied all the odds and is meant to be here; maybe she will be a teacher one day. After all, it runs in her blood.

-Katie Kinder

CHAPTER SIX:

If We Build It, They Will Come

Derrick Sier

In a blog post by Practical Theory entitled "Free the Hallways" the author says:

> *According to school architect and author of The Third Teacher, Trung Le, over 35% of the square footage of the average school are in use less than 5% of the day. The hallways. The reason for this is that the institutional design that schools most resemble are prisons.*
>
> *Think about it — we move kids from cell to cell, we monitor their coming and going whenever they leave their cells at anything but the designated time, often giving them a pass so that other adults can know immediately that the student is allowed in the common space, and many principals are taught that the secret of success as an administrator is to clear the hallways as soon as the bell rings at the start of class, and most schools give three or four minutes to get from class to class, no matter how big the campus is or how crowded the hallways get at the change of classes.*

And we wonder why kids feel like school feel like prison.

If we want kids to feel that schools are more human places, let's start by making every space a learning space, every space a social space. Let's free the hallways.

Let that sink it. A third of the space in our schools aren't even used to their maximum capacity and ability. It's not even close. It's significantly disproportionate and the little steps we've made toward multi-using the space is marginal. I'll say it for the people in the back and on my tippy-toes from the mountain top, "IT DOESN'T HAVE TO BE THAT WAY!"

Hallways don't have to be sterile wormholes that rush students from one dull learning experience to the next. Hallways don't have to be navigated by walking on straight lines painted on the floor. Hallways shouldn't have to be guarded and monitored by folks who count down the minutes to when they gain back control of rowdy rule-breakers and dis-regardant pubescents (I definitely made up two words there).

A third of the space in our schools is severely underused and can absolutely be transformed into experiential, creative and connective spaces! In the Fall of 2020, "We Are Teachers" posted 25 ways schools could transform their hallways from blah to bangin', from meh to magical, from tragic to transcendent, and from tolerable to tantalizing. All it required was a small budget, a big heart and a creative mind. On that list were effective and impactful ways to help the classroom spill into the hallways and continue to engage students in explorative and exciting ways.

First, that means there are things schools can do to their hallways which engage students without present teacher involvement. That simply means, the students will use the hallway experience to occupy themselves. These are even projects on which the schools and the students can partner. Ask the students what they would like to see on the walls and if they would like to help re-create the space.

Second, it's not only the space that isn't being maximized. The time is also being underutilized. A current student and web-editor-in-chief, Hope Rosa, says in her school newspaper, there are five primary things for students to do during their passing period: use the restroom, study, nap, party and have a little me-time. Now, four of those seemed pretty standard, but the party suggestion really caught my attention. She says, "Our campus is the place to be if you're looking to let loose at 8:15 on a Monday morning." What kind of administration and teaching staff turns up on a Monday morning? What group of teachers are bringing in Friday afternoon energy at 8:15 on a Monday morning? Well, let me tell you. These are the kinds of administrators and teachers who value the students and their learning environment so much, they will sacrifice their preferences (assuming they want to have a quieter and slower morning) for the wellness, welfare and advancement of their students.

Third, last but not least, even if there isn't any music or interactive decorations on the walls and hanging from the ceiling, students should feel and remain connected in their in-between times and spaces. At no point in time should a student feel disconnected from their supportive environment nor feel the need to unplug or disconnect. Allow me to elaborate.

Outside of the academic rigor or topic, what is happening in a class where the student feels the need to unplug or disconnect? Are their classmates being rude and insensitive? Are their teachers being negligent and coarse? Is the learning environment not conducive for learning? For whatever reason a student may want to disengage, as an education professional, that should now become my focus. I'm not talking about the need for a change of scenery or a breath of fresh air. I'm talking about the inability of a student to feel comfortable everywhere.

In research presented by Learn Alberta, being able to maintain appropriate behavior in school hallways allows students to have positive interactions with others. While this research is extremely sterile and provides little room for nuance, the heart of the data shows that in order for students to have increased chances of positive and healthy interactions, 1) the environment must prioritize positive and healthy interaction and 2) school administration/ teachers must do their part in making sure that environment is established and remains active and intact.

Hallways are more than avenues to get from one place to another. They are also opportunities for learning, exploring, creating, connecting, expressing and discovering... about things, subjects, each other and most importantly, themselves. And in the words of greatest sports films of all time, Field of Dreams, "If we build it. They will come." Let's pour more energy, focus, creativity and liberation into the way our students navigate their schools. It's a small, yet wonderful opportunity to highlight the journey as well as the destination.*

-Derrick Sier

---

* http://www.thethirdteacher.com/
http://practicaltheory.org/blog/2013/07/01/free-the-hallways/
https://www.weareteachers.com/school-hallways/
https://nordicnews.net/11406/cheeky/five-ways-to-kill-time-during-passing-periods/
https://www.learnalberta.ca/content/insp/html/hallways.html

CHAPTER SEVEN:

The Intern Is Watching

Taylor Upchurch

After fourteen years in the classroom, I decided it was time for a change. I loved where I was, and loved the people I worked with. Some of my co-workers became my life-long best friends. It was one of those friends who saw something in me, and was fairly relentless in encouraging me to take the step into school administration. After years of thinking, 'I am going to miss my students and I will not be able to build relationships like I can in the classroom,' I made the jump.

Luckily, I was able to secure an administrative internship in a district just east of Oklahoma City. The superintendent there happened to be one of my professors during my Masters program. This internship was uncommon though. It was designed so that I would be in three different schools over the next year. I was assigned to a high school for three months. I would then move between two middle schools. Two days here, two days there, and alternating Fridays. I did not know at the time that this would be such a huge bonus for my growth in becoming a school leader. Who else gets to learn from more than ten administrators during a year-long internship?

My first day to report was July 28th. School would be starting in three weeks, but planning and scheduling must be done before teachers report. I was excited, nervous, and had no idea what was in front of me. The night before work I pressed my slacks and laid out a tie. Overly-eager, I arrived early. I was the first one to arrive and as I sat in my car and watched other staff members roll in, I realized that I was way over dressed. How embarrassing! The first thing I learned as an intern is that on reporting day, school leaders are still in summer mode. There is no need for a tie.

I spent the next three months at this high school working for an amazing leader. If you were to walk into the building looking for the school leader, you would know immediately who it was; Dr. B was proud of her building. She wanted nothing but the best for her employees and students. Dr. B was also a leader that wanted me to learn. She did not caudle me or place me as an assistant to an assistant. She valued my input, and taught me a lot. She threw me into one instance where an educator I was working with needed some extra guidance or a gentle reminder and nudge to start moving in the right direction. Dr. B told me it was time to write an improvement plan and meet with this staff member. Mind you, I am the intern. I stared at her. "Um, are you sure?" and it was unequivocally, "YES!" Dr. B had the confidence in me to do the job and she also wanted me to learn by doing. She knew this was the only way to really learn. Dr. B gave me hard jobs and put me in positions that I was uncomfortable with, and I knew in the process I was learning. My first stop on the road to becoming an administrator was fantastic. I could write another chapter entirely about each of the assistant principals I was able to work alongside, one who would become my boss two years later. They became great friends; I am not sure I'll ever find another team that is as funny and fun to work with than them. We laughed a lot, and that is a tip for anyone reading this who works in education. Laugh. Laugh with kids, with coworkers, and at yourself.

The second half of my internship was splitting time between two middle schools. I taught for thirteen years in a high school. Middle schools are a special place. If you have ever worked in one, you can read this and swell with pride and also giggle at the same time. My middle school tour allowed me to learn from two different head principals and many assistants. Noah was the head principal at one of the schools. Morning duty, hall duty, cold days of recess, Noah did not skip his assigned duties. It would be easy as a head principal to drop those duties for "more important" things. Noah figured if he was asking his assistants to do it, he would be there also. I stowed that away in my mind as I watched him in awe; I, too, wanted to be that kind of leader. Wednesdays and Thursdays sent me north to my second middle school of the week. Here, I was able to work with amazing administrators who all taught me something different. The assistant principals taught me that discipline and consequences can look different and still work for the overall good of the school. One AP approached student behavior with an open mind, something I try to emulate in my current position. One was a pro

when it came to meeting with teachers and having those tough conversations. He was matter-of-fact. He had a plan to help the teacher become better, and he followed up with their progress, good or bad. His ability to sit down with teachers that needed a little extra guidance is something that I struggle with, and I know my weaknesses. Let's not forget about the lead learner of this school, the person who bought her own broom and dustpan so she could clean the halls while she was out of the office. Mary made sure her school was presentable. She did not mind doing the dirty work. I once witnessed Mary crawling under a portable building to find something a kid had stashed. No kidding. The head principal in dress clothes, crawling on all fours, through a tiny crack in some metal sheeting, only to find an empty airplane bottle of vodka. We could not stop laughing that day looking at our principal covered in dirt holding a tiny empty bottle of vodka.

The bonus round was an elementary school. The last time I'd been a part of an elementary school was in 1995 as a student. I've not taught elementary, observed in an elementary, nor am I certified to be an elementary administrator. One evening I received a phone call from someone who told me that I needed to report elsewhere in the morning. One of the elementary schools was down their head principal and an assistant. I stepped into a role

I knew nothing about that was being led by the other assistant principal. You would have never known though. Carol was running this school and leading me, the new guy, very smoothly. And, this was the week before Spring Break and the week Covid shut down the world. What I will remember about this experience is that Carol must have had a great boss. She knew the mission of the school. That is something a school leader teaches anyone working alongside them. She was prepared and had the school running smoothly. I remember her conversations she had with the staff before leaving. I remember how she planned to get medicines back to families once the school shut down. Carol was the leader of a building in a tough time and she led well.

My internship in this school district was everything I could have asked for. I will never get the opportunity to learn from that many people in such close quarters ever again. I can read a book or go to a conference and still partake in meaningful learning, but it's not the same as being in the hallways with the people doing this job day in and day out.

-Taylor Upchurch

CHAPTER EIGHT:

Hallway Leadership is Coined

Heady Coleman

As I think back to when the term 'Hallway Leadership' was coined, I remember it this way, Taylor Upchurch and I were talking about his role as a principal and his approach to leading in his new role. Taylor went from teaching in the classroom to leading as a principal, so I was curious to know what changed for him.

His approach:

I specifically talked to Taylor about how he was winning as a classroom teacher and he talked about the power of being in the hallway as his students were entering the classroom. He saw how it was making a difference for the students, and how they approached learning during his class.

I felt like I could also hear Taylor talking about how it made a world of difference in his relationship with his students by meeting them in the hallway vs his students filing into class and finding their teacher behind his desk.

I was recently hanging out at a school, and I noticed that as the students were changing classes, I didn't see many teachers in the hallways at their doors greeting the students as they came in, and I started thinking about my friend, Taylor.

I believe in the power of greeting, not only in the hallways as students enter into the classroom, but also at all events i.e. birthday parties, concerts, church, grand openings, weddings, and any other event that might need a friendly face. The right person greeting at an event can be a game changer for the environment or special occasion. I created a whole side hustle based around greeting for events. Some might even call me a professional greeter! That's how much I believe in it.

When Taylor told me about his approach, I was locked in.

Then I asked Taylor what this looked like in his new role as a principal, and he began to explain that his approach was much the same, but his target was now the teachers and the students. He would greet them as he walked the hallways.

Hallway Leadership sounded a lot like what I call "Hello Leadership." My 'Go Win' approach is so much more than a slogan. 'Go Win' is being consistent in doing the right things that allow me to achieve the wins I have defined for my life, so that I can live out my greatest story.

My Hello Leadership, Go Win, and this newly coined phrase 'Hallway Leadership' approach boils down to five right things in my opinion.

1. **Help others achieve their wins.** Leadership for me is about serving others. Out of serving others, I gain influence. With that influence, I want to guide people in the right direction. This could be their dream or a role they are playing to help someone else achieve a win. My question is always; How can I help? Helping others is a great way to make a positive difference in the world. Whether it is through volunteering, donating, or simply lending a hand, helping others can bring joy to both the giver and receiver. The act of helping others can be incredibly rewarding, as it can provide a sense of purpose

and connection. It can also help build relationships, strengthen communities, and create a more just society.

2. **Encourage people every chance I get.** Encouragement is a powerful tool that can help people feel more confident and motivated to reach their goals. It can be as simple as offering words of support or providing constructive feedback. Encouraging others can help boost morale and foster a sense of belonging. It can also help build trust and strengthen relationships, as well as promote collaboration and problem-solving.

3. **Listen to others more than I talk, and take action of what I hear.** Listening is an important skill that can help us better understand and empathize with others. Listening with an open mind and without judgment, can help build trust and create a safe environment for sharing. Listening can also help us learn from others and gain new perspectives. By actively listening, we can show respect and appreciation for another person's ideas and feelings.

4. **Learn with the mindset to teach.** Learning is an essential part of life, and it can take many forms. Whether it is through formal education, informal learning, or simply through life experiences, learning is a valuable tool for growth and development. Learning can help us gain new skills and knowledge, as well as open up opportunities for personal and professional growth. It can also help us become more aware of our surroundings and better understand the world around us. One of my favorite ways to learn is from others. The best way to learn from the people you get to lead is by being able to ask great questions.

5. **Observe those you lead.** Observation is a powerful tool that can help us gain new insights and understandings. By paying attention to our surroundings and taking the time to observe, we can gain valuable knowledge. Observation can also help us become more aware of our own thoughts and feelings, as well as those of others.

It can help us become more attuned to our environment and better understand the world around us.

Being in the hallways is a great place to observe.

Hallway Leadership to me has this same approach. This could be the difference between a student being successful or not. Simply, being out in the halls vs sitting behind your desk when students come through those doors.

I believe in this type of leadership. Go Win!

-Heady Coleman

Heady Coleman is a friend, father, pastor, encourager, greeter, community builder and your number one fan. The scope of his personal and professional capacity astounds me. His willingness to engage, give, create and lead is an example for anyone wanting to impact humanity. From his current and past work in the non-profit service in Love OKC to his community building with Shipwreck Talks to his people development with #GoWin to his entrepreneurial empowerment with GuthrieAmerica to his business development as Chamber CEO to his community building with Made Possible By to starting NORTHCHURCH Guthrie - take a breath - the guy does it all with grace, humility and a smile. He's the most encouraging person on the planet too and was once voted the Citizen of the Year in Guthrie Oklahoma? It would be to your good fortune to connect with him. Your life will be enlarged!

CHAPTER NINE:

The Visible Leader

Charles Williams

There is a very common conversation that I have with individuals who are unaccustomed to my leadership style. It goes something like this…

Guest: You are a very difficult person to get in touch with.

Me: Am I?

Guest: Yes, you are never in your office when I stop by or call.

Me: That's because I'm rarely in my office.

Guest: Really? Why is that? Don't you have things to do?

Me: Of course I do! And that important work doesn't happen *in here.*
It happens *out there.*

In nearly every position that I have held since I started working in 8th grade, I was focused on those in leadership roles. Knowing that I wanted to, one day, hold a similar position, I made it a point to study how they maneuvered and interacted with those around them. Overtime, I began to notice trends signaling various leadership styles and traits that identified the types of leaders that I admired and those that I despised. Of the numerous characteristics, one in particular stood out to me.

Good leaders must be visible leaders.

Visible leaders set the tone for their organization by modeling the behaviors and attitudes they want to see in their team.

During our recent playoffs, a student asked if I would be attending the game. I responded that I would be in attendance with an enthusiastic, "yeah." He asked if I would be willing to modify my response to an enthusiastic, "hell yeah." Chuckling, I politely declined while another student pointed out that I would not do it because I don't curse. I shared with the student that I, like all people, occasionally use "foul language," but they would never hear me do so.

Working in a school, especially a high school, one will hear all types of creative language used. Okay … profanity. While I recognize that this language may be commonplace within social settings or other locations, I am not comfortable with it being used in professional or academic settings. In fact, I have made it my personal mission to never allow my staff or my students to hear me curse. With so many barriers and obstacles impeding the advancement of African-American and other minority populations, I do not want the misuse of language to be an additional impediment as the excessive use of profanity is often seen as an indicator of lesser intelligence and lower social class. Regardless of the validity of these perceptions, I prefer to prepare my students for the world in which they will enter, not the one that they should be entering, and thus I model an expected behavior that they, in turn, learn to shift while in my presence.

Visible leaders build trust and credibility when they are present and engaged by demonstrating their commitment to their team and show that they are invested in their success.

Part of my morning routine is to do sweeps of the building. I begin by making a round while teachers are setting up before students have arrived, using this time to check the status of the building and to check-in with staff. This allows me to simply say good morning, inquire about a weekend or prior evening event, or inventory a supply request. An hour or so later, I make the same rounds so that I can check-in on our students, preemptively address any concerns, and drop off those needed supplies. Throughout the day, I try to check in on each classroom at least once giving me the opportunity to see the amazing work that is happening, and to be available if I am needed for additional support. Both the staff and the students have come to expect these visits and they are not seen as a form of micro-managing, which is absolutely not my intention, but instead a sign of my desire to see and help them succeed.

Teacher evaluation systems have, in many ways, developed a culture in which classroom visits are not perceived as supportive, but purely judgemental. With such high-stakes, the possibility of tenure or the loss of a job, it is no surprise then that teachers and staff often do not feel comfortable sharing their vulnerabilities or struggles with the person responsible for determining their overall effectiveness. This, however, does a disservice not just to the teacher but to the students in the classroom as well who are directly impacted by a service that is not being performed at the highest possible level. If we, as leaders, want to ensure that our students are receiving a high quality educational experience and that our teachers and staff have the capacity and capability of delivering those results, then we must be willing to move beyond occasional judgments toward ongoing support.

Of course, it is easy to talk, or in this case write, about the importance of being a Visible Leader but it may not always be so clear on how to actually become one. Consider these suggestions:

1. **Schedule time to be out of your office.**
    Most leaders rely heavily on a calendar to keep track of their numerous meetings and deadlines. This same calendar, and those awesome built in reminders, can also be used to schedule classroom visits. Take some time at the end of each week to review your calendar for

the upcoming week. Find one hour each day to spend outside of your office. This could include lunchroom visits, classroom visits, or simply walking the halls and the grounds of your campus.

2. **Get creative with consistent communication.**

Newsletters are a traditional way of connecting with stakeholders, but are they always the most impactful or effective? During the pandemic, I started weekly video blogs that contained much of the same information and noticed that my engagement skyrocketed. Consider using a communication app such as Class Dojo or Remind that allows parents to connect via SMS on their phones. Regardless of how you choose to communicate, find a way that best suits the needs of your stakeholders and be sure to send out information on a regular basis. This consistent flow of communication will help you and your message to better be "seen."

3. **Be intentional about building connections.**

Meetings seem to be an integral part of our professional lives. So much so that we seem to have meetings about having meetings. These sessions, regardless of how productive they are, often lack in building relationships as they are focused on processes and procedures with the hope of delivering results. An organization cannot function on results alone. Consider taking time to foster connections by scheduling an outing with your staff or holding a talking circle where people can openly share their thoughts, feelings, and feedback. Demonstrating a personal level of care and concern allows your followers to be seen and your participation helps to drop the veil that often masks leaders.

-Charles Williams "The Velvet Voice of Education"

Charles Williams has served as an educator for nearly 20 years as a teacher, an assistant principal, and a principal for students in grades K-12. He also serves as an equity advocate with the Equity Offices of the City of Chicago and the Chicago Public Schools. As a reflection of his dedication to doing this important work, Charles also hosts "The Counter Narrative Podcast" and co-hosts an edushow called "Inside the Principal's Office." Through his consulting company, he is a best-selling author and a highly sought after workshop facilitator and keynote speaker. He has also, affectionately been coined "The Velvet Voice of Education."

CHAPTER TEN:

Excuse Me... Do You Have A Minute?

Marcus Belin

I love being out and about in the school building and connecting with kids and staff. Who doesn't want to take time to connect with the people we serve every day? Over the past few years, we have become so focused on the challenges that have plagued schools post-pandemic. We have also fought for every minute of our day because we never know when it will be taken away. So we spend our time planning, making sure the calendar is up to date, and logging minutes checking the ever-growing "To-Do" list to ensure we have important items accounted for. Then, it's time to take to the halls of the school and talk to kids, faculty, and staff.

Upon entering the hall you inevitably hear, "Excuse me, do you have a minute?" It's almost like being at a party and you hear the record stop. What runs through your head is a ton of different thoughts.

- "Are they going to hit me with something I can't answer right now?"

- "Are they going to tell me something that will change my day?"

- "Are they going to talk for a long time?"

And so many more questions come to mind, and these questions have so much power to shift the day. I will tell you, as a school leader, I am not a huge fan of this question. Sometimes I look around or am focused on the next "thing" on my schedule, and I realize that maybe the most important "thing" is standing right in front of me. It could be a kid, a staff member, or a visitor to the building; who knows? Most importantly I must remind myself that we have to make time for the people we serve.

There are a few things to remember as an administrator that can help you value the time you have with the people you serve.

- **BE RESPONSIVE** to your students and staff. This is important because it helps to establish a positive and productive learning environment for everyone. It shows that you value their needs and concerns and are willing to listen and address them promptly. This can increase student engagement, job satisfaction, and motivation for everyone leading to improved performance and better student outcomes.

- **EMPOWER VOICE:** Allowing teachers and students to have a voice can empower them and give them a sense of ownership over their education. Giving intentional space where you can listen and allow everyone to be heard supports a positive learning environment. Listening to voices impacted by the decisions of schools and school leaders can provide new insights that can improve the teaching and learning experiences of staff and students.

- **BE YOU:** There is a human element to the job in which you serve kids. Some of you are like, "DUH…that's obvious!" However, it is vital for people to see you as a human being with the ability to listen, understand, and value people.

We are always busy with the work we do regarding the livelihood of our students and staff. Teachers can only teach if they are heard. Students can learn that their voice is not valued. So the next time someone stops you in the hallway and asks you the question… "Do you have a minute?" Don't be upset, make an excuse, or find another hallway to travel. Engage in the conversation for a couple of minutes. It may make someone's entire school year because you did one of the most critical jobs of leading a school and that, my friend, is listening!

-*Marcus Belin*

Dr. Marcus Belin is a principal, motivational speaker, and podcast host of the Unapologetic Leadership, a podcast designed to tell and share the stories of leadership and the passion behind the work of being an educator. He is the 2021 NASSP Digital Principal of the Year, a Class of 2021 ASCD International Emerging Leader, NASSP Board Member and Past President of the Illinois Principals Association. He is passionate about creating learning environments that foster social-emotional support for kids, leveraging the integration of technology to expose kids to the world around them, motivating educators, and challenging the status quo of education. Dr. Belin is the husband of an amazing wife and a father to 3 beautiful children who are destined for amazing things.

CHAPTER ELEVEN:

Put Your Oxygen Mask on First

Shari Gateley

For those of us who have been on an airplane, we've heard the safety speech by the flight attendant, "In the event of a loss of cabin pressure, put your mask on before assisting others." This is because a loss of cabin pressure can lead to hypoxia - an inability for your body to continue to function in a normal manner. This safety measure is one that none of us question. We know we have to be able to breathe in order to help those around us breathe. In fact, we accept this as a perfectly acceptable and reasonable expectation. Yet taking care of ourselves before taking care of others seems diametrically opposed to what we have told ourselves servant leaders do - serve others at all costs. Servant Leadership, coined by Robert K. Greenleaf, is first about serving first. However, somewhere along the line we have morphed the idea of servanthood into total abandonment of oneself for the sake of others. While this comes from a place of well-meaning intentions, I would argue that serving others while not taking care of ourselves leads us to a state of metaphorical hypoxia where we will develop an inability to serve others well, function normally, and make the best decisions for those we desire to lead.

Servant leadership at the cost of oneself is an easy trap to fall into. In schools, our job is urgent. If we fail, kids fail. If we succeed, kids succeed. We put such an intense pressure on ourselves because we love the kids, families, and communities we serve deeply, and want nothing more than to open the door to equity, opportunity, and access. I, too, entered the profession to make an impact, to empower, and to inspire, but the more I watch teachers, administrators, friends, and colleagues run out the door because of very real, very understandable burnout, the more I want to scream "we are doing it all wrong!" We need to, no we *HAVE* to, listen to the safety message from flight attendants. The only way we can do the work in a sustainable and meaningful way is to put our oxygen masks on first. That's right, we cannot serve others well if we don't take care of ourselves first. For myself, this means I have to surround myself with people who get it, a solid dose of therapy, and learning to manage my time in a way that allows me to do the work that is important and not be consumed by tasks that can wait.

FIND YOUR PEOPLE AND ASK FOR HELP

Leadership can be both rewarding and exhausting - exhausting in different ways the higher you move up. It can also be incredibly lonely. When I first considered the jump into school leadership, I remember a colleague telling me how different it is to "sit on the other side of the desk." It didn't take me long to realize the truth in that statement. Quickly I realized the higher you move up, the fewer people understand exactly what you are going through, the decisions that have to be made, the messes you have to clean up, or the information you are privy to. One of the best things I have done as a leader is finding my people- people who understand the job, understand the pressure, understand the difficulty and the nuance, and people who mentor me along the way. And, for the sake of all the people I love, I also realized that the burden of being "my people" can't just be on them. There, at times, has to be some separation for the sake of keeping those relationships healthy and whole. Just as our students' trauma can wear on us, our own stress, frustration, and hard days can wear down those who love us and make the job an all consuming part of our lives.

There is also something uniquely special about developing a network of people who "get it." When I reach out to my people, they tend to know exactly what I need at that moment whether it be a listening ear, advice, or a simple "yeah, I feel you." Knowing I'm not alone in this really difficult human work can be the breath of fresh air that allows a moment of grace, peace, and clarity. These people have also become a safe group to ask for help because the reality is we all need it, we cannot do it alone, and we are better when we work together.

GET A THERAPIST

For some reason, as servant leaders and educators, we absolutely understand that those we serve need to be emotionally healthy. Putting our oxygen mask on first means we must first make sure we too are emotionally healthy. Education is a helping profession, it's human business, and it means we get the joy and the heartache impacting and doing life with kids, families, and communities. Being in a helping profession not only requires a significant giving of your time, energy, and self, but it also means learning about and responding to the hardships others go through. In some cases it also means being situated in pockets of an immense amount of trauma, racism, poverty, bigotry, xenophobia, and more. Some of us, even those of us with an immense amount of privilege, also have generational and childhood trauma we carry into the profession. We cannot, and should not, expect ourselves to carry the emotional baggage with no outlet or no release, and we cannot,and should not, think we can successfully help others work through their trauma without working through our own.

Therapy has been a saving grace for me, and a moment every other week I have come to believe is as important as exercising, eating right, and drinking enough water. It is the time I learn to process, breathe, re-center, and actually learn to lead better. Through therapy, I've learned how to navigate difficult situations from a place of empathy, vulnerability, and shared understanding.

IS THE FIELDHOUSE ON FIRE?

One day as I was sitting at my desk debriefing with one of my assistant principals at the end of a very long day, I got a phone call from another assistant principal. He said, "So I think the fieldhouse is on fire." I started laughing, clearly this was a joke based on the craziness of the day, but he said, "I am actually being serious." Immediately, I knew exactly what to do and jumped into action. We have trained for this, it was an urgent situation, and we have very systematic responses we train and practice for in these situations: evacuate the fieldhouse, call 911, let district leaders know, and go from there.

As I moved up in leadership, a mentor said to me "separate what is urgent from what is important. If everything is urgent, you will never get to what is important." It took me a minute to really figure out what that looked like in the day-to-day. I am a fixer, and when someone steps into my office I have a sincere desire to help "fix" whatever situation they bring to my desk. I want them to feel important and supported, so we can accomplish what we set out to. However, one thing I learned pretty quickly is the more "urgent" I make things that are not urgent, the less time I have to do the work that is truly important (and the work that brings me joy).

Very few things in education actually require an immediate decision or response. While something may be very important to another individual, it cannot and should not derail the important work that drives our WHY or the vision and mission of our school. I've learned to ask myself, "is the fieldhouse on fire?" when a situation arises, and if it is not a situation that requires an immediate response, I give myself permission to schedule time for that later so I can stick with doing the important work. I've learned to say "I'd really like to give this my undivided attention, but I cannot right now. Can you send me an email and we can find a time to sit down and discuss this when I can be fully present?" The win of this is that it actually allows me to be more present, more engaged, and more authentic when things need my attention.

Education is absolutely the foundation of strong communities, and schools are the places where change begins and hope is realized. The best schools and classrooms are run by people who, because they love those they serve, put their oxygen masks on first.

-Shari Gateley

Shari Gateley is a high school principal in Oklahoma. She started her career as a high school English teacher where she earned the honor of being her district's Teacher of the Year and a top 10 finalist for Oklahoma State Teacher of the Year. Shari received her Master's degree from the University of Oklahoma and is a current doctoral candidate at OU. Her research focuses on the school-to-prison pipeline and the use of restorative justice in schools. Shari is the proud wife to Joshua and mother of two incredible boys, Griffin and Jordan.

CHAPTER TWELVE:

Hitch your Wagon To a Star

Andrea Sifers

Since 2009, in the years that I have had the pleasure of being an educator, I can think of no less than a million (okay, maybe not a million) buzzwords that have come and gone and ebbed and flowed with pendulum swings. Some that immediately come to mind...fidelity, pivot, self-care, learning loss, differentiation, and my personal least favorite: rigor. Just typing it makes me throw up in my mouth a little bit. Some words however, have a little more sticking power for the long term. One that immediately comes to mind is servant leadership. Despite this word originating more than fifty years ago, it's a buzz word that, well, deserves a lot of buzz. Its effectiveness speaks for itself. In the business world, companies that are run with a servant led leadership style are more likely to keep their employees (HELLO teacher shortage!), outperform their competition, and create more servant leaders. Why wouldn't we want that for education? A "do as I say, not as I do" command and control leadership isn't just as out of style as skinny leg jeans are to Gen Z, but let's face it, it's ineffective. Some of the most admirable people in history could be defined as servant leaders. Martin Luther King Jr., Mother Theresa, Mahatma Gandhi, and one that may ring a bell to you, Jesus Christ.

One of my most vivid memories with students regarding servant leadership was a fundraiser for my elementary school, a delicious spaghetti dinner. All hands were on deck this evening with teachers serving our stakeholders in exchange for their ten dollar bills to purchase things for our classrooms. At the end of the evening, while everyone was cleaning up, a couple of fifth grade boys came up to talk to me while they were waiting on their moms to finish talking, imagine that. I had noticed there was a pretty significant mess between the tables and had swept up the mess as best I could, and was coming back with a mop bucket filled with soapy water. As I started mopping up the remaining spaghetti sauce, one of the boys said, "Mrs. Sifers, why are you mopping? You're the principal, just tell a custodian to do it." As I continued with the job that needed to be done, I just looked up at the boys with a smile and simply said, "Jesus washed feet." to which they replied "Uh…what does that have to do with mopping the cafeteria?" When I responded with, "If Jesus wasn't too important to wash feet, then I'm not too important to mop the floor." As those words sunk into those boys, they both gave a slight nod and walked away. I thought they were going to find their families, but instead they both walked to the counter to get a soapy towel and helped the staff clean tables. That was one of those defining moments in my career that didn't need to be broadcasted across Facebook or Twitter for a pat on the back, but definitely one of those that changed my perspective on the type of leader I really wanted to be. I struggled with whether I wanted to include this story because I think the key points of servant leadership is doing things not for the recognition, but because they need to be done and serving the people in your care is one of the greatest forms of love and respect I can think of. But with that being said, when Katie Kinder asks you to write a chapter in her new book and tells you that you have to tell all the things, you tell all the things.

At its core, servant leadership means being a servant first, and a leader second. It means taking on the responsibility of others' needs. It means making the students and staff you serve your first priority. We all know as educators that different fires burn hotter at different times on different days, but at the end of the day if your people are going home feeling like they're not supported by someone in the arena with them, I don't know that your priorities are straight. Servant leaders have innate and almost a natural desire to serve those around them. They empower the people trusted in their care and remove themselves from a leadership pedestal in order to achieve whatever shared vision they have. Leading from the back, while putting others before you so your people feel empowered in whatever they do, that is true leadership.

Over the last four years of leading a school, a great school, might I add, there have been many opportunities to serve my people, both adults and the tiny humans. On professional development days, I've been known to make my awesome husband (who is a great servant leader himself) drag my Blackstone grill up to school, so I can make sure my staff doesn't have to worry about breakfast when they're already rushing around, making sure their own children are taken care of while they come collaborate on a great education for other people's children. One particular morning in February, I remember doing this, along with more members of our admin team, and it was so cold the scrambled eggs were freezing before we could pour them on the grill. Turns out pancakes take twice as long to cook when it's 26 degrees outside. At a school my size, Baby Bear size, you know, not too big, not too small, just the right size, we are sometimes met with struggles that plague schools on either side of the scale. One week a few years ago we didn't have a single custodian in the building. It was the perfect storm of Covid hitting one, while another was out recovering from surgery, and a third had traveled across the county to help with the birth of a grandchild. Things were still taken care of that week. Now I will admit the building was not nearly as clean as when our fantastic custodial crew was all accounted for, but did I make sure that I pulled on gloves to clean toilets, take out the trash, and make sure the carpets got vacuumed? You better believe it! That was not a thing that needed to be added to my teachers' plates, and something I knew I was capable of doing for them and for our students. There are so many opportunities to serve your people: take a lunch duty, so someone else can get an uninterrupted lunch, watch a class, so someone can go to the bathroom, when the buses run late (I bet that never happens at your school…) send your people home so they can spend time with their families and wait with the kids still waiting on the buses. I try to think of it like this: if you're going to ask someone else to do it, you had better be right there beside them putting on your boots and getting ready for hard work.

I would be remiss if I end this without mentioning one of the best ways to become a servant leader; surround yourself with servant leaders. One of my favorite teachers ever, who I completed my student teaching with years ago, had a saying, she would tell her students often, "Hitch your wagon to a star." That has stuck with me all these years across a variety of settings. While it's a great idiom to use in lieu of 'you are who your friends are,' I choose to use it most in a leadership sense. I have been so lucky to be surrounded by so many amazing leaders. My Superintendent and friend, Scott Farmer, is one of the greatest servant leaders I know. That man will jump in and help with anything, at any time, and is usually two steps ahead of thinking of ways to help people before there's even anything to help with. Fort Gibson is blessed with an amazing school board filled with servant leaders who make decisions in the best interest of kids, and you will see any one of them around campus all school year long, supporting and cheering on not only our students, but our staff as well. The administrative team I work with is equally as amazing. They will serve lunches, drive students home, cover classes; you name it, they will do it. Find these people in your life and hold them close; hitch your wagon to those stars.

-Andrea Sifers

Andrea Sifers is the principal at Intermediate Elementary within Fort Gibson Public Schools. In 2022 her school achieved Model School status under her leadership. Before moving into administration, she taught at Fort Gibson, Sallisaw, and Wetumka Public Schools. In 2015, she was named a Rising Star by the Oklahoma State Department of Education. Since 2014, she has been providing professional development to educators all over the country through Great Expectations. In 2021, Andrea won the Oklahoma Administration Award from the Oklahoma Literacy Association. She has been district teacher of the year at both Wetumka and Sallisaw Public Schools. Andrea has served on the Executive Board with the Oklahoma Association of Elementary Schools Principals since 2018. Her proudest accomplishment is being someone that kids can learn to depend upon with a sense of understanding. Andrea's husband, Dusty, is an administrator at Tahlequah Public Schools, and her son, Cooper, has aspirations of being a paleontologist.

CHAPTER THIRTEEN:

The Safety and Security of a Counselor's Heart

Shay Omokhomion

"The first and most important choice a leader makes is the choice to serve, without which one's capacity to lead is severely limited."
- Robert Greenleaf

Hallways tell a fascinating story about the spirit of a school. It expresses the time of year,seasonal school events, sports, auditions for school plays, and flyers for school dances. The zeal and pride of the school are tangible. Walking down school hallways gives an essence of what the students feel day in and day out. It's the place where they make their first friend; It's where they see their secret crushes in passing. It's where friends gather for more than half of the time allotted for passing periods. The place where they can engage with their favorite teachers and staff.

Hallways allow the students to grow and connect socially in ways no other area of the school can. Time spent in the hallway is short and done in spurts, yet it's impactful because students can be their authentic selves.

Servant leadership gives us a framing and accountability to help nurture and foster their authenticity and autonomy; It's developed through modeling, committedness, and community. How we invest in our students directly affects how they see themselves and the abilities they possess.

Servant leadership would prepare me for one of the most fulfilling endeavors of my career. During the Pandemic in the Fall of 2020, I accepted a school counselor position at a local middle school; this also happened to be the largest inner-city school in the metropolitan area. As I prepared to embark on this new journey, I pondered the characteristics that aided my ability to build healthy and genuine relationships with the prior students and school communities. I thought about the most meaningful moments I remembered having with my former students and colleagues. I started looking for recurring characteristics in all of those moments. As I sat and thought about the possibilities, my excitement to engage with my students grew. There was only one dilemma: There were no students in the building.

Confined by remote learning, the hallways were empty for months-except for enrolling students, which became a welcomed anticipation. As time continued to pass, the ardor I initially felt started slowly leaving as the absence of youthful faces laughing and walking up and down the hallway became more painstakingly apparent. The silence was loud yet still. Day after day, I saw engaged teachers lose their spark and sizzle. They, too, missed the interaction and in-person engagement with the students. It was clear that no matter how overwhelmed teachers, administration, and staff may feel about our job or how excited we may be about our much-needed time off- the students' energy is the school's pulse. That pulse is what breathes life into a school.

The longer the students stayed away, the weaker the pulse became. It made me realize how much our students shape who we are as educators; how much we need their involvement to challenge ourselves to be our best for them. Above all, the most important thing I learned is that just as much as we needed the students in the building; they not only needed, but also desired to be in the building with us. I was inspired by my students because, instantly and without warning, their whole lives changed. Our new reality exposed us to the many challenges we didn't know how to navigate as a society then, yet, many students still showed up, ready to figure it out.

Struggling to adjust to the new normal, several of my students would email me messages expressing how lonely and confused they felt. The dozens of messages I received spoke very little about school work, but deeply about how much they missed being in school with teachers and friends. Witnessing my students' hardship due to the Pandemic left me feeling helpless. The resilience they embodied taught me an important life lesson about leadership- it first began with mindset.

John Quincy Adams once said, "If your actions inspire others to dream more, learn more, do more and become more, you are a leader." When the school district announced the end of distance learning and a return to brick and motor, I knew I had to identify a quick and non-invasive way to welcome our students back to the building. It had to be something that would create rapport and build relationships. I knew the readjustment of returning to the building would come with challenges. Even still, I was determined to identify a strategic, yet authentic way to engage with my students. I wanted to do something to let them know we missed them as much as they missed us. I spent weeks thinking of impactful ways to engage interpersonally with them. That's when the idea hit me, one of the most effective ways to create healthy engagement is through consistency. I chose consistency as the foundation for relationship building because it breeds predictability, builds trust, and cultivates safety. Furthermore, I wanted to see the effects of this one simple, yet complex practice. I was going to engage in one consistent primary practice of greeting my students in the hallway each morning as they came in for breakfast. I would welcome them with high energy and optimism to get them excited about the school day.

As students entered through the door, I would, in the most obnoxious voice I could muster, gleaming with excitement, belt out "GOOD

MORNING!" as they passed by. Initially, some of my students would laugh or walk by without replying. Yet, as time passed, they went from no words to acknowledgment to reciprocal communication. Some of my students wanted distant hugs (due to COVID-19), and some wanted distant high fives and fist bumps. As I made this a daily routine and my consistency of showing up grew, I could see the excitement on many of my students' faces as they lined up to enter the building. Seeing students so excited they couldn't keep still created a contagious energy that was hard to ignore. Some students would tell me how stupid it was to stand there and greet students every day... as they stood there and greeted students with me.

Andrea was one of my students who could not understand how the simple gesture of greeting students daily would make a difference in her classmate's behavior and engagement. I invited Andrea to stand and welcome her classmates with me, and she did. Each day, she saw me with a positive attitude and paused to readjust my focus and mindset when I didn't feel so positive. Andrea saw me extend grace to students and staff on their bad days. She witnessed me speaking to her peers respectfully and not asking or expecting something from them I had not done or was not willing to do. She saw me exercise accountability and self-awareness, not just with students and staff, but with myself.

One morning, as we stood in our designated spot in the middle of the hallway, Andrea looked at me and said, "I get it, Ms. Shay," as she nodded, and I nodded too. John C. Maxwell says it best, "people do not care how much you know until they know how much you care."

From that simple act, I gained the trust of many of my students over time. The consistency of showing up to the same spot every day, with a smile and a silly dance, excited to see them- even after difficult days- made it safe for my students to connect with me.

As time passed, I could detect which of my students were having a difficult morning just by their facial cues and body language alone. Establishing rapport with my students allowed them to feel safe with me, and allowed me to pull them aside and speak with them when those rough moments occurred. My morning greetings also allowed them to see my personality outside of "just" being an authority figure- we were able to humanize each other. My willingness to meet them where they were, on good days and bad days, made them feel safe with me. And because they felt safe with me, they trusted my leadership.

The moment I knew my hallway leadership made an impact was when my students would inquire about my whereabouts on the days I could not greet them in the morning. They expressed how seeing me in the mornings made them feel safe. It showed when I offered them guidance or direction. Not only were they open and receptive to what I had to say - they felt encouraged to try. When my students felt supported and protected, it allowed me to work with them on behavior modifications and aid in classroom management.

Dedicating myself to this took a lot of work and effort. As a school, we had our share of problems and difficulties, as all schools do. Not all students were open or receptive to relationship and rapport building. I had to learn to be okay with that, so long as they knew the option was there if they ever chose to act on it. I noticed that even with those select students not interested in high engagement- mutual respect and trust were still created. James Baldwin said, "Children have never been very good at listening to their elders, but they have never failed to imitate them."

The intentional practice of servant leadership is essential because its purpose is not to control but to guide, support and nurture. This work requires action more than words. Once our students can trust the consistency and predictability of how we treat them and engage with them; they will inevitably grow to value what we say- even when it's difficult for them to accept. Every child desires structure and wants to be intrinsically acknowledged for who they are. It's not about grandiose gestures, but about the development of character. It's making the space for them to exist within their agency and helping to nurture the gifts and talents they all possess.

Doing so ensures we establish a more solid future by shaping and molding well-rounded innovative humans in the present with love.

- Shay Omokhomion

Shay Omokhomion was born and raised in Oklahoma City. She attended The University of Oklahoma, where she received a Bachelor of Arts in Psychology with a minor in Sociology. She also attended Langston University, where she received a Master of Science in Rehabilitation Counseling. Shay has been a practicing therapist for over six-year and received her full licensure in 2021. She does individual and family therapy primarily with African American adolescents and adults in the areas of Anxiety, PTSD, and Depression. As a middle school counselor, Shay focused much of her effort on assisting students and colleagues with emotional regulation and re-acclimation to traditional school settings and standards. Shay is also a Relationship Development coach, aiding clients in developing inclusive and practical tools that foster healthy interpersonal skills in their respective relationships. Shay has a daughter, who she loves dearly. In her free time, she enjoys spending time with family and friends, doing creative things, and traveling.

CHAPTER FOURTEEN:

This Is What The Teachers Want!

Erin Patton

I never wanted to be a principal. A teacher's life was the life for me. I loved getting to meet MY group of students and their families each year. I loved building relationships with them, bonding with them, loving on them, listening to them, laughing with them, hurting with them, fighting for them, and growing with them. Each year, I deeply fell in love with my small, little chunk of the school.

Over time, I came to realize that the rest of the school was filled with other teachers in their own classrooms who were, just like me, loving on their little chunks of the school.

Each school needs a strong leader to unite these individual chunks into a cohesive team. Someone who sees the big-picture and works to support their teachers, as they are doing everything they can to take care of their students. I am grateful that there are people out there who want to be principals. Because, for real....the thought of the ENTIRE school looking to me to call the shots and to make sure each and every thing is running smoothly for students, teachers, staff, and parents makes my heart instantly beat faster. The anxiety starts to creep in. Yikes. No thanks. Thank goodness for principals!

While in the classroom, I was in the same elementary school and had the same principal for all fifteen years of my career. My principal, Mr. B, showed me support, care, and trust. His leadership was, in large part, why I stayed at the same school for so long. Unfortunately, I know that this is not the case with every teacher. Since being out of the classroom, I have been working with fellow educators and former teachers on a project called "Relate Then Educate." We love teachers and want to provide a place to share teachers' stories. Through meeting and interviewing many teachers on our podcast, at conferences and workshops, and on social media, we've gotten to hear many stories. And, boy, have we heard it all! There are some teachers who are a part of incredible communities within their schools who feel supported and looked after. Too often though, we hear of horror stories of what this principal did or that principal said. There are a lot of teachers out there who are aching for good leadership in their school.

So from my experiences in the classroom, combined with the many experiences I've heard through interviewing teachers, here's a list of some of the top things we want in a principal:

- Models Healthy Boundaries
- Builds Trust
- Cultivates a Healthy Culture
- Prioritizes Growth
- Shows Appreciation

MODELS HEALTHY BOUNDARIES

Teachers, if left to their own devices, will never stop working. You know it's true. And the same could be said about our principals. Healthy boundaries and clear expectations modeled from the top down is crucial. Seeing this from our administrators allows us the freedom to not become enslaved to our work. Work doesn't define who we are as living, breathing human beings. It's something that we do. And since we are more than our jobs, should we not be investing our time in more things than just our place of business?

We interviewed two teachers who co-teach in a 1st-3rd grade classroom in a public Montessori school in Oklahoma. We conducted the interview in their classroom. Throughout the course of our conversation, the teachers mentioned several positive things about their principal. We had to meet this woman! When we asked if they could introduce us to her, they laughed and told us that she was long gone. She leaves everyday by 4:00 and on her way out, she goes through the hallways, encouraging as many teachers as she can to get outta there too!

Clearly, she values her teachers. She sees them as complex people with real lives outside of the classroom. Daily, she models what she expects from her teachers and displays a healthy work/life balance.

BUILDS TRUST

Let's start with the assumption that teachers are showing up to work each day to do the best by each of their students. Sure, there are teachers who will require some extra care and attention to get to this place. But the norm is that there's a school full of teachers who want to be there, who earnestly want to teach, love on, and encourage each one of those kids in the building.

As trained professionals, teachers want to feel like our principals trust us to get what needs to get done, done. Feeling trusted by my principal gave me confidence in my lessons, allowed me to take risks and try new, revolutionary things in my lesson planning, and encouraged me to continue building strong relationships with my students.

Principals, have your teachers' backs! This means you step between the teacher and the parent when necessary. Don't let us get eaten by the wolves when we should be a team. Once the situation is less dire, have an upfront, one-on-one conversation with your teacher. If there is an issue in which the teacher's actions could be improved, communicate with them on how they could've handled the situation better. Strong leadership includes elevating those you are leading through trust, intervention, and conversation.

CULTIVATES A HEALTHY CULTURE

You can FEEL the vibe of a school with a healthy culture. As soon as you walk in, you know it's there. It's cohesive. The teachers, the students, everyone is operating within a team mentality. Contribution and sharing are expected within the staff and competition is limited. When teachers work well together, the entire school benefits. A good principal values and appreciates the uniqueness each of their teachers bring. They aren't threatened by their teachers' personal successes or accolades because that success is good for the whole school!

In another interview, a teacher from a public school in Missouri told us about her incredible kindergarten team of teachers. They fully back one another and recognize that it takes all of them to support each of their precious kindergarteners. Not only are they supporting the students within their individual classrooms, they also assist and care for all of the kindergarten students and teachers. If one teacher is struggling with a certain student, perhaps a change of scenery in another room could help. No judgment. No problem. Afterall, they're a team!

Teachers, we must understand that, like us, our principals are overworked. They also keep getting more and more added to their plates. Let's extend some grace because we all know what that feels like!

Our career path can be so very hard and incredibly gut-wrenching at times. Not having a cohesive team is isolating and lonely. This career path can also be some of the most fun and rewarding work you'll ever do. The benefits of a healthy school culture are vast and often determine how long a teacher will or will not stay at their school.

PRIORITIZES GROWTH

A good school prioritizes academic growth. A superior school also prioritizes personal growth. It's important to care about your teachers' *real* lives, not just their Mr. or Ms. selves. Taking time for yourself, spending time with the people you love, and doing things that fill you up is restorative and energizing. It allows teachers to grow into healthy versions of themselves who are then ready and able to show up for their students each week. A teacher who has a healthy work/life balance has a much greater chance of staying in the career and growing to be a master teacher, instead of leaving within the first few years. Keeping your evenings and weekends free of school and even taking the occasional mental health day should not be shamed. It should be encouraged and expected.

While we're talking about growth… just because "that's the way it's always been done" is not a reason to keep doing it. You're missing out on some amazing opportunities for growth and improvement if that's your mindset. Look around, take a deep breath and ask, "what isn't working?" Check in with your staff. I bet they have some thoughts. Having a willingness to change and grow is necessary in an effective principal and teacher. Stay curious and be willing to be wrong. It's all about learning and growing! At least that's what we tell our students, eh?

SHOWS APPRECIATION

Teachers are no different than anyone else. We want to feel valued and that our efforts aren't going unnoticed. It's draining to continue giving and giving when no one seems to care.

I'm grateful I had a principal who was aware of how important it is to show others we appreciate them and are recognizing their efforts. It certainly meant the world to me. Mr. B was great at showing his appreciation to his teachers. Sometimes it would be a quick email that he saw our class in the hallways working hard on their science projects. Other times it was a note in our mailboxes to quietly thank us for our hard work. There would often be a public shout out in a staff meeting or staff email. Whatever it was, the point is, we were being noticed. Seen. Mr. B made me feel the same way I hope I made my students feel.

Finally, teachers and principals, if you're not feeling the support that you need or if you aren't feeling like your school is a good place for you anymore, know that you have options. You do not have to stay there. Where you are now and what you've experienced so far is not the only way. Each school environment is different and there are phenomenal principals out there who do lead their schools beautifully. If you do not see these qualities at your school, understand that they are out there. Teachers often stay in this field because of their students. What if wonderful leadership was a reason too? Work to create an environment in which your employees look forward to coming to work.

Dear Teacher and Principal, you are more than your work. You are complex, nuanced human beings who must prioritize the *real*-life you. You're worth that!

You are worthy.

You are valuable.

You are loved.

-Erin Patton

Erin Patton is the Social Media Director, podcast host, and a speaker for Relate Then Educate. She spent fifteen years in elementary classrooms teaching Science, History, and STEM. Connecting with her students has always been the most important thing in her classroom. Erin is inherently curious and knows that by listening and having a willingness to understand others, we have the invaluable opportunity to learn and truly grow.

Relate Then Educate

CHAPTER FIFTEEN

The Cell Phone Wand Heard Round The School

Katie Kinder

"Technology is a tool and we must use it, but we must never overuse it! Technology cannot replace the lasting impact a caring teacher can have on the lives of children!"

Smartphones aren't going anywhere, so what do we do with these distractions during the school day? Listen, I have teenagers, and I want those teenagers to have their phone on them, so they can call me if needed. I can track them. Yes, I said it! We have moved beyond any home having a landline. It is almost ridiculous to think of our Gen X selves holded up in our closets, phone cord stretched to the max, so we could gossip with our girlfriends into the night. We have phones in our pockets, and they are glorious. We are all addicted to our phones, but as adults, we understand the value of a face to face conversation; we understand when the phones must go up, and full attention must be given to the task at hand. Guess what? Our kids do not have the fully developed prefrontal cortex to be able to discern these types of situations. When I train educators all over the nation, this is their number one issue. My advice: Ban the phones during the school day. Yep! We know the kids have them, but they are not to be seen, and in 99 percent of schools I go to, the kids are 1- to-1 with chromebooks, ipads, or some other sort of school issued device. If the students already have the ability to use their school device for educational purposes, the phones should be put up!

As the principal in the building, you can either help enforce this for your staff or not, but I will tell you that when I worked for administrators that banned the phones from the top down, the years were smooth. But, when I worked for admin who said, "we ban the phones," but they really didn't enforce the rule; it was much more difficult. Not only did the kids in their care learn that the school 'procedures' or 'rules' were negotiable with phones, but with everything. The principals weren't standing by their word, and the kids took advantage. 'What else can we get away with' was the mentality around their buildings.

A couple of years ago I worked for a principal who effectively banned the phones. It was the first, and most important initiative he put in place when he became the new principal. Every kid had a working locker, and the expectation was that the phone was in the locker. We knew otherwise of course, but since it was a top down initiative, I never saw a phone! Like ever.

He even went as far as buying a 'wand.' A cell phone wand that could detect when a phone was near. The kids didn't know it, but that wand from Amazon was a fake. It looked real, and he ran around campus with it, and he stood at the eighth grade hall with it, turning around any student that thought they could get away with having the elusive phone in their back pockets. He didn't play. And guess what? At lunch, our kids interacted, and learned to play appropriately. Would it have been easier for the principal to have allowed the phones at lunch? Yes, but he did what was relentlessly best for kids and their social emotional development. He didn't do what was easy for the adults on lunch duty: him and his other assistant principals. No, he did what was right for kids, and he had the power, authority, and character to see out this initiative, and our test scores went up, referrals went down, and kids were learning how to interact and collaborate correctly.

France has a new law in place in which kids are not allowed to even have their phones on campus. It is the law. What have they seen as a result? Higher test scores, less behavior issues, less referrals, less distractions, and learning environments that allow kids to thrive. Education research shows that even if a student's phone is turned off and turned upside down on that student's desk, their IQ still goes down by ten points because all they can focus on is how many notifications they might have on that device, and my friends, that is the antithesis of our jobs.

With phones, I understand as a teacher that I must be both loose and tight. What does that mean? If a kid comes to me in a panic needing to message or call their mom/dad/guardian, I always let them step outside and do so. Ask permission, send the quick text, and put it back up; it is based on trust and the family classroom. Also, a privilege that can be taken away if abused.

Listen, I love my phone; I teach my kids that people use social media as a highlight reel or to promote their businesses. I enjoy TikTok, and playing Solitaire; I can scroll mindlessly for hours before I realize half of a day has passed. I can binge watch a show on Netflix and turn up two days later full of cheese, and unaware about the passage of time. We all do this. However, when I'm collaborating with team members or I'm in a room with another creative, I put my phone on silent, and I throw it into my purse, and I can be in community with others in a real and authentic way. This is a skill, unfortunately, that we must teach. It may never be a law in your area or you may never purchase fake cell phone wands for your admin team, but what can you do?

-Katie Kinder

CHAPTER SIXTEEN:

Hallway Hugs

Derrick Sier

It was the summer of 2001. I was 19 years old and working for the Salvation Army's Boys and Girls Club. During the school year, we would have after school programs, but during the summer, we had those same kids all day and all summer. I was old enough for the kids to know I was one of the adults in charge and young enough for them to sometimes forget I wasn't one of them. It's an interesting dynamic. Especially when working with youth. There's the age where you're too close to them to be taken absolutely seriously. Then there is the age where you're close to them, but removed enough to be considered cool and an authority figure. Then there's the age where you could have kids their age if they're young enough. Then there is the age where you are too old to be considered relevant and should definitely not be doing their dances or speaking their language. While I've navigated all of those successfully, in 2001, I was in the first category and had to consistently prove myself as an adult all the while the kids were constantly testing my gangsta!

In my training, my supervisor told me over and over, "Because of your age, you'll have access to their heads and hearts, but don't let that determine how you use your hands." In this case, "hands" was a reference to discipline and redirection. We had to do that often. And while the discipline and redirection was most times verbal, sometimes our actual hands were needed. I struggled with this. I understood the kids. It was summer time and they were not at home with their parents. They wanted to be free and have fun. We also wanted them to experience that type of environment, but within certain boundaries. When those boundaries were tested, my loving hands were unshackled from my head and heart and I went into action.

On this particular day, the kids were in the middle of activity rotations. Swimming. Game room. Movies. Gym. I loved basketball and when given the choice, I always chose the gym. In the gym with me was a new young lady named Katriana. She liked to be called Kat. As we did with all of the kids who entered the after school and summer programs, the staff reviewed Kat's profile and discovered she was a foster kid who was on her fourth family in less than a year. We were warned of emotional outbursts and a tendency to rely on physical violence to communicate and convey frustration. On this day, Kat became frustrated.

While playing basketball, Kat was accidentally hit with a ball and assumed it was intentional. She reared her head, set her eyes on the young man who was shooting on the same goal and sprinted toward him with her fists balled. I was fortunate enough to see the incident develop and rushed to stand in between Kat and the boy. In an attempt to get to the other person, Kat tried to run through me. My response…a hug.

The harder Kat fought. The harder I hugged. She squirmed. I hugged. She kicked. I hugged. She swung. I hugged. I eventually moved her, full hug, into the hallway where she absolutely broke down. She yelled and cried. She repeated over and over, "No one hits me! No one! No one!" She scratched herself; she hit and kicked the wall. She even pulled at her hair; she tore her clothes. And yelled and screamed some more. The entire time, I stood there…in the hallway…away from the other kids… and let her get it all out.

Eventually, she got tired, and leaned against the wall. I walked over to her to say something corrective and inspirational and before I could say anything, she fell into my arms. By the time she was ready to rejoin the group, my shirt was wet with her tears and Kat was smiling again.

You see, hallways are known to be loud and noisy and jammed packed with energy. They can be decorated and colorful or plain and sterile. But rarely do we talk about the healing components of hallways. They can be quiet spaces where students and teachers gather their thoughts. They can hold the tears no one will ever see. They can hold secrets no one will ever hear. They can echo the deep and gathering breaths of anxiety. They can be the practice booths for first speeches and first kisses.

Hallways are dynamic. Hallways are healing. And if you don't believe me, ask Kat.

-Derrick Sier

CHAPTER SEVENTEEN:

Be The Nancy In Your School

Taylor Upchurch

I am going to go out on a limb and guess that there are more hallways than administrators in your school. Too many places to be, meetings to hold, and students to usher to class. A good leader knows they can't be everywhere at once. So what does someone like Nancy do in this situation? Nancy is intentional in seeking out leaders in her school to help carry the load. I was lucky enough to be one of those people.

Nancy has spent over thirty years in one same building as a teacher, an assistant principal, and head principal. Multiple generations have learned from this wise educator. She is an Eagle to the core. Nancy's approach to leading her school could be summed up in four questions she often asked each day:

"How can I make this easier on you?"

"What do you want to learn before leaving here?"

"How ya doin'?"

"Did you watch Yellowstone this week?"

Nancy brought me into her office early during my first year working with her. Her question to me that day, and multiple times throughout the year, was, "What do you want to learn how to do today?" Nancy would continually tell me that I would someday lead my own school and she wanted me to be prepared. Years of experiences were at my fingertips like a library of "How to" books. I recently read through my text messages between her and me. One text followed a time in her school when she was hiring a new employee to take her role. It was my turn to remind her, "You can exhale deeply and know that the culture you have created will continue on. Good leaders train people to become good leaders." I am forever grateful for the time I worked alongside Nancy because I know she was in the business of creating leaders.

Nancy led her school in this same way. She was always out of her office meeting with teachers and checking on students. It was her way to spread the leadership. Nancy followed a trickle down approach. She built up her assistant principals to turn around and build up her teachers to turn around and build up her students! When we talk about this thematic idea of hallway leadership, Nancy instantly pops into my head. As the year went on, I would watch as Nancy handed off responsibilities to staff members. Some she trusted from years of working together, others she wanted to challenge and grow. You could feel the cohesiveness of her school. Teachers were aware of the mission of the school. Students were proud to be there and bought into this mission, and Nancy was the reason.

Nancy was very intentional about the staff members she invested and in turn relinquished more responsibility on. One staff member Nancy entrusted was the student leadership teacher. Many people around the state know and respect this teacher. She is one heck of a leader. The first time I saw this particular teacher was at a state student council conference where she was a speaker. I do not remember many details of her speech, but I do remember looking over at her students. There were some crying listening to their teacher and some screaming and cheering her on. It was a beautiful thing and one of the reasons I chose to apply to work at this school years later. She made an impression on me then and would again one day while we were both working together. I was asking her about one of her freshmen who had recently gotten in trouble. I was worried that this student may not be the best fit for a leadership role. My mind was focused on behaviors. Her mind was focused on results. This teacher set me straight and let me know that she gives them a whole bunch of responsibilities knowing that some will mess up. But she also assured me that this was exactly how they learned. She had confidence in her students that I could not see. She trusted them knowing they would make mistakes and she was alright with that. She exuded so much confidence that our school hosted the state student council convention a few years later. I can only guess that this teacher learned some of her methods from Nancy herself.

Two students who were in this leadership class ten years prior have since returned, and are now teachers. They both did not go to college to become teachers, but when looking for careers, they remembered how great their experience was at our school. Nancy hired these two former Eagles and immediately placed them in leadership positions. Nancy saw the energy and enthusiasm that Rick and Jamie brought to the school, and wanted that to spread to others.

As a school leader, when you see something good, you highlight it; you call attention to it. Nancy was great about this. It is a simple practice, but it helps lift spirits when things are hard. I loved seeing these two teachers flourish in their first year as teachers. They were excited to be at work. They welcomed students to class with a smile, and they attended students' games and performances. That is something that is not taught in college courses. It is something that is built through relationships. I believe that Rick and Jamie saw this from their teachers and principal when they were in high school. In a way, Nancy grew her own teachers. What a legacy!

One year the school was in need of a science teacher. I had a former athlete and student message me asking questions about becoming a teacher. Hailey was one of my favorite athletes to coach. Educators aren't supposed to have favorites, but we all know that we do! We have favorites; we just try not to make it obvious. Hailey was one of the top three funniest kids I have ever been around. She was also part of the team that gave me my nickname, Rev. Hailey had a science background and had been working in a lab testing Covid. I mentioned to Nancy that we should interview Hailey. I knew that Hailey was someone that would fit at this school. The principal, Nancy, was all about hiring a "fit." It was super important to her that staff members contributed to a positive culture. Nancy hired Hailey and a year later promoted her to head volleyball coach. She continued to be intentional about who she placed new teachers next to. She was intentional about the mentor Hailey would work with. I really do appreciate Nancy giving Hailey the job and placing her near positive influences in the building. We always want the best for the people we care about and serve.

The more I think about this school, the more I see that Nancy's greatest characteristic is that she trusted her employees. If you want a strong, positive culture within your school, I'd suggest you, the principal, begin to trust your staff first. As a lead learner, I encourage you to be more like Nancy.

-Taylor Upchurch

CHAPTER EIGHTEEN:

Walk Around A Lot

Adam Welcome

Having spent the last 20+ years working in public education as a classroom teacher, school and district office level administrator, and also having worked with 300+ school districts around the country the last five years, I've seen a lot of different scenarios.

The number one most impactful way to lead - is to simply *walk around a lot*. You can't know where you need to take your organization if you don't know where it is, and you can't do this from sitting in your office.

The simplicity of *walking around a lot* is just so undervalued and underutilized, I really think more leaders need to implement daily walks around the school.

Now I've seen organizations do data walks, curriculum walks, behavior walks, instructional round walks, relationship walks and those can add a lot of value and provide lots of different types of information that can definitely help move everyone in the right direction.

But when you simply just walk all around your school, that's when you can find all those little things that need your attention.

1. Walk
2. Talk and ask questions
3. Look
4. Listen
5. Engage

This isn't some type of technical program or training device that someone can sign up for, it's really just walking and talking and looking and listening and engaging.

Here's an example:

I recently had the opportunity to be a substitute Principal for a school that needed some administrative support, which is a unique job and also allowed me to 'not' have to focus on the typical demands and responsibilities of a school leader.

So I walked around a lot!

And it was such a great reminder that regardless of your situation, everyone can walk around a little bit more to go just that much deeper. Each of these five characteristics (walk, talk, look, listen and engage) can be done independently of each other, but they're way more powerful when done in conjunction.

Don't overthink it, just walk and talk and look and listen and engage.

There was a big problem with trash on the playground after lunch recess. The trash problem was hundreds of plastic water bottles. All the water fountains around school had been turned off because of Covid, so the kids were given plastic bottles of water during lunch. They would bring them to recess after they ate, and then the lack of garbage cans on the playground would result in bottles on the ground.

I found out about this problem because I like to walk around during lunch when the kids were eating, but also walk on the playground while they were playing, and then walk after lunch recess was complete when the adult yard supervisors were 'cleaning' up the playground.

They had bags and bags of these small plastic water bottles, filled to the brim and it just all didn't make sense to me. Now you can't just walk around, you have to also ask questions and look and listen and engage.

Me - "What's up with all these water bottles on the playground?"

Yard Supervisors - "The kids are given bottles of water at lunch and most don't finish drinking them so they come on to the yard and then we clean them up."

In my head I'm thinking of about three to five solutions for the bottles and all this garbage that the adults are cleaning up. Fast forward two days and there were ZERO water bottles on the playground.

Turns out the vast majority of the kids had barely any water left in their bottles when they left the lunch tables. And after 'looking' and 'listening' for ONE day as the kids walked from the lunch tables to the playground, the rest of them drank the remaining water as they walked.

They didn't even need the bottles on the playground. Which means we didn't need more garbage cans for the kids, we just needed them to not bring the water bottles to the playground in the first place.

So that's what we did. And we figured this out by walking around a lot.

As a former Principal for seven years, I can tell you that a lot of the decisions I made every single day didn't have anything at all to do with education. But the more you walk around and just make things easier and smoother at your school or organization as a leader, it's going to make those educational decisions that much better when you do have the opportunity to make them.

Start walking. Keep walking. Have a walking contest with other leaders in the district. And just see where your feet take you for the kids!

-Adam Welcome

Adam was Principal of the Year for his region in California, a 20 to Watch for the National School Board Association, guest blogger for EdWeek, NAESP magazine, and many other publications. Adam consults and works with many education companies as a way to improve their product for others. Adam is passionate about technology integration with all educators and a huge advocate of social media and connecting with educators from across the globe. Adam makes it clear that kids come first and has preached the message of Team Kid for many years. He is the cofounder of Kids Deserve It and an author of four books: Kids Deserve It, Run Like A Pirate, Empower Our Girls, and Teacher Deserve It. Adam has an amazing wife with two children that keep life at home exciting and active. Adam also loves to run and has completed 30 marathons.

CHAPTER NINETEEN:

From Goals to Action, Being the Thermostat in the Hallway

Tron Young

Hallway Leadership is not the sum of the things that you do. No, it is who you are. Your thoughts, actions, beliefs, and values. All of these things build the thermostat from which you lead. School leadership is like setting the thermostat. Just setting the thermostat is not enough if the thermostat does not operate as it is supposed to and be the conductor from which air flows. So is the role of school leadership, you are setting the tone, culture, climate, and environment for which teachers are able to educate and students are able to learn.

Does this mean that everything rises and falls on your leadership? Yes, that is what it means. Your students will only be able to achieve as high as you believe that they can achieve. Your teachers will only take risks and be innovative in their teaching practices as you are willing to inspire them to be, and give them the freedom to take those risks. That type of learning environment is only able to be set if the leader is actively involved in being the leadership thermostat. So ask yourself, what is your leadership thermostat? How do you set your leadership thermostat? How do you adjust your leadership thermostat?

It took me a while to understand this concept and many days of frustration. Why? Because being a school leader means that you often move from fire to fire, crisis to crisis, and majority of the time these situations are not ones that you have developed. In the days, you were a teacher, you only had to worry about your classroom. As a school leader, you have to worry about the front and back cover, every classroom, every teacher, every student, club, program, activity, etc. In this reality, I understand that we do not make a positive impact or change, in our office. It is done in the hallway. So let me help you understand and move to being the thermostat in the hallway to create a school that moves from seeing other people's work on social media and wondering how they do it, to actually being in the hallway creating moments of impact.

The first step is to develop and know the goals you have as a school leader for the type of school you want to have. Your leadership goals as a building leader are the anchors from which you will lead from. You have to set goals for the type of school you want to have. This is different from school improvement goals that target specific areas of growth that derive from scores that indicate who may not be meeting or exceeding expectations based on some state or local assessment. Your goals as a building leader is the foundation from which you lead from and evaluate the work you do. If you have not set them, ask yourself what do you want your school building to feel like, look like, and sound like? What do your classrooms feel like, look like, and sound like? What do you want your hallways to feel like, look like, and sound like? The questions will either help you set or evaluate your goals for the type of school you want to have.

Hallway leadership means you have to be where the kids are. Far too often you hear students say, "I do not ever see my principal, or I don't even know if the principal knows my name." If you are going to be a leader that inspires students' tomorrow to be brighter than their today, you have to be where the students are throughout the day. You have to leave your office and not wait for the moments to come to you, but you have to build those moments. For example, how do you start your day? Are you in your office responding to emails, talking to your secretary, or completing the paperwork? If any of those sound familiar, relax, we all have been there and done that. What you have to ask yourself is, when starting your day like that what temperature are you setting for yourself and your school?

Imagine, if every morning you are at the main entrance of your school greeting students as they enter. As you are greeting students, you are calling students by their first name, or talking to them about the sporting event or concert from last night. What leadership thermostat are you setting? What does this interaction display about your leadership and what model does it set for your staff? What if in the morning, you are in the cafeteria with your lunchroom staff helping them serve breakfast to the students once a week? I wonder what your students would think about you performing this role? How would your lunchroom staff react to this interaction? During the passing periods, walk the hallways not looking to correct students' behavior as a disciplinarian, but to connect with students as a thermostat leader. Look to inspire students that have their heads down and feel ignored. Show them that you see them, they are important, and they matter. Acknowledge the student who often comes to your office to see you for the wrong reasons. Go see that student in the hallways or their classroom, so they know that you value them as a student and not just as "that kid."

When you are where the students are, you get to see who your students are. You are able to see how they interact with each other inside and outside the structure of a classroom setting. You build emotional and social capital that you will be able to use in the moments that you need to motivate or correct a student. You have a face to put with that picture in your yearbook as you are creating visions, missions, and direction for your school. You will be more informed of the types of professional development that will meet the needs of who your students are, and not who you wish they were.

Your presence in the hallway and classrooms will be a model from which your staff can visibly see. You are not leading from the back. You are standing front and center modeling the school culture you want. When you lead professional development, the credibility that you have is not just based on your position that you hold, but on the knowledge and impact that you will have. Furthermore, the professional development provided will be aligned to the building goals which are connected to the leadership that you have demonstrated in the hallways and classrooms.

Hallway leadership is all about being the thermostat. It is not about what you can inspire others to do, not about the mission and vision you can put on a piece of paper, it is not even about the test scores that are assigned to your school. Hallway leadership is all about being visible. It is about how you model, lead, interact, speak, motivate, connect, and do for others to set the thermostat for a school culture that innovates, motivates, and inspires your students and staff to achieve beyond their wildest imagination.

-Dr. Tron Young

Dr. Tron Young has 17 years of combined experience as a middle school teacher, elementary principal, and middle school principal. He is the building principal at Joseph Arthur Middle School in the Central 104 School District in O'Fallon, IL. He is the 2020 Illinois Middle School Principal of the year and Illinois NASSP National Distinguished Principal of the Year. Dr. Young is the founder and organizer of the Illinois Grow Summit to grow, retain, and recruit more educational teachers and leaders of color. He is the founder and host of the Be The Thermostat Podcast. Dr. Young is also an adjunct professional at Southern Illinois University - Edwardsville. He has been a featured speaker and presenter at local, state, and national conferences. He emphasizes the importance of goal setting, school culture, teacher professional development, staff motivation, and leadership coaching. He has been a motivational speaker at middle and high schools, speaking on perseverance, making good choices, setting goals, and youth leadership development.

Dr. Young believes you have to do the things that others do not think to do to get the results that others are not able to get. Be the Thermostat and Not the Thermometer!

CHAPTER TWENTY:

Beware The Red Flags, Principal X

Katie Kinder

This is a compilation of stories told in break rooms, lounges, twitter chats, and whispered in closed door classroom meetings across the nation; it is a reminder, an alert, and a warning to "not be this guy."

PRINCIPAL X

We have shared many stories of some amazing leaders who exist inside of the education system to this day, and our hope is that you find yourself working for and being in community with servant leaders. But, we wouldn't be doing this book justice if we didn't forewarn you about the leader you shouldn't be, so welcome to this bonus chapter entitled: Principal X.

Principal X says all the right things; X says things like, "We do what is best for teachers, and we are stronger together, and we do what is best for kids, and we have a community school where parents are welcome in, and there are procedures in place to keep everyone safe!" But seldom does X ever actually follow through with action. The words are empty, and soon the staff, the kids, and the parents know that Principal X means nothing they say.

Principal X can be found hiding in her office or he will send out a mass email to the entire staff to discipline only one teacher while every teacher in his care wonders if she was talking about them. It is vague and problematic.

As I've circulated the country and done research on my own, here is a list of red flags as told by educators everywhere.

1. Students don't know who the head principal is because she is rarely seen in the hallways. Red Flag.
2. Teachers feel insecure because the principal is constantly on the cameras to see which teachers are talking to each other. To take it a step further, after the principal sees a teacher go into another teacher's room to talk, the teacher gets an ominous email stating they are not allowed to go into other teachers' classrooms for advice. Red Flag.
3. The leader doesn't care about teachers as people or students as people. He only sees data and test scores. Red Flag.
4. An educator is told by a student that another student has a weapon, and as the teacher frantically tries to get ahold of a principal, there is no answer. Red Flag.
5. When a situation is dire and a student is in danger, a teacher alerts the principal of the situation and the leader blows it off as if it doesn't matter. Red Flag.
6. When the principal is unengaged, disappears a lot, evades questions, and is all around hard to find. Red Flag!
7. When a school leader is not forthcoming with their lives, they are refusing to be vulnerable or practice vulnerability like we do with our students; it is hard to feel like a family this way. Red Flag.
8. When a school leader rages at teachers and makes them feel afraid, Red Flag.

9. The principal seems to play favorites, but the favorites are not the school innovators or best teachers in the building, and she seems intimidated by other strong females, Red Flag.

10. Saying we need to practice self care, but having meetings every single day after school adding more to teachers' plates. Red Flag.

11. No positives ever coming out of the mouth of the leader or a refusal to acknowledge teachers and students as people in the hallway. Red Flag.

12. Principals who gossip about staff members in earshot of others. Red Flag.

Listen, as educators, principals, superintendents, and school personnel, we know that this job isn't easy. Being the leader for everyone while sacrificing yourself is not something we would ever want for you or for your teachers. We are out here doing the best job we know how to do, and you are too. I have seen first hand a brand new principal get better and better over time. I have seen first hand a brand new teacher get better and better over time; I have seen students get better and better over time. You see, I think the important part to remember is that we should all continue to strive for that growth mindset, admit mistakes, apologize when necessary, and lead with empathy, but if you ever wonder why your staff isn't being forthright about what is happening in your school, take a glance at the Red Flag list, and look inward. Putting a mirror up is sometimes the nudge you need to get better, so keep getting better.

Teach on, beautiful principal warrior; we are rooting for you.

-Katie Kinder

CHAPTER TWENTY ONE:

She is Her! The Principal

Katie Kinder

She was the brand new principal at a school her district was planning on shutting down. Her district gave her the job of bringing up enrollment or else. In one of the largest crime infested neighborhoods, in one of the largest cities, surrounded by low income housing projects, sat her elementary school in which she was their only hope of keeping the doors open. This is her story.

There was a fight every day when she started. She ran from fire to figurative fire every second of every day at this school. The building itself was structurally falling down. The ceiling was concave, the air and the heat did not work, but her district wouldn't give her a dime to fix it until enrollment was up and test scores too. She felt hopeless at times. She did daily internet searches on how to discipline appropriately; she held onto research and books and experts about how to turn this school around. Slowly, but surely, she began to turn the tide.

She hired well and got rid of teachers who were not for kids. She protected her teachers on a daily basis. One day she was alerted that an irate parent was screaming and yelling at one of her teachers outside. She would not stand for it. She stepped in the middle of this fray and sent her teacher back inside. The mad mama screamed, and screamed, and screamed some more until the principal said the mama needed to leave, and guess what that parent did? She threw an entire Big Gulp of Dr. Pepper directly over the principal's head. This story became legend around the school, and the principal started to earn her stripes.

Going into her second year as the principal, she knew she needed to serve the entire community, and not just the students. She asked any and everyone with money to help her school. And they did! She implemented community dinners, and churches around the city would cook for the community. Most of her student population came from the large housing projects that surrounded her school, and she learned that most of her families didn't own cars. Transportation came down to riding three different buses to get to a Walmart ten miles away for groceries. Nevermind the money it took to get there, and there were only so many items they could get because they had to carry it onto the bus and then back home again.

This principal implemented a garden in which each family had a plot of land they farmed and grew their own food, and she got the funds from many generous donors to build a grocery store on the property run by a charity keeping the cost down for her families. The community started protecting the school, started to garner self worth from this amazing school, and guess what? Enrollment skyrocketed. The district finally gave the green light to build a brand new school right in the middle of the housing projects, right next to their new community garden, and right next to their brand new grocery store that sat on the campus of the school grounds.

After two years of ceilings literally and figuratively falling in on kids and teachers, termite infested classrooms, a beautiful new school was built. This principal had literally saved the school. Closing the doors to this school would now be absurd because this school had grown from about one hundred kids to 420 children walking the halls at her school. This school became the hub of the entire community.

The principal knew the community needed their school. Saturdays, the gym was full of basketball games, pokemon tournaments, and birthday parties. She implemented a food pantry, a clothes closet, and made sure that if someone needed the school to be open on Friday nights for community dinners, or Sundays for family potlucks, she made sure the building was open to serve her families.

She grabbed a hold of initiatives that made her school soar in every area one could possibly imagine. She used Positive Behavior Support (PBS), she got uniforms donated for every student, she had a family meeting every morning with the entire school called, "Rise and Shine," she created a foundation for just her school to further fund needs that arose in her school community. She got presents donated to every child, every Christmas. She turned three school adopters into twenty four businesses, churches, and community members that regularly supported her school. She started a mentor program with over 250 people from the community signing up to be mentors for her students. She used STAR, students thinking and acting responsibly. Her school was deemed an "A+" school. She doubled her test scores in her tenure as principal, but she never did it for the scores. She did it for the people, for the teachers, for the kids.

She is: Cindi Hemm, my mom.

-Katie

Want the rest of the story? Search "Miracle on Southwest Boulevard," and read in awe of this amazing lady I'm proud to call my mom! She did it all with positive deviance and a joyful heart while she said, "sometimes, it is better to ask for forgiveness than for permission."

CHAPTER TWENTY TWO:

Be Visible

Katie Kinder

"The number one intentional act of the building principal must be visibility with presence. Live in the classrooms, hallways, and student gathering spaces. Ask questions of students and staff. Learn from their answers. Support and challenge alongside the people."
- Bethany Hill, Joyful Leaders

I will admit to never being a building principal. I saw the work my mom did, and wholeheartedly believe in her philosophy, and I have consoled and comforted many friends who were posted in this position, but I have never wanted that job. It is a hard job, and the building culture goes by way of the leader, full stop.

However, as an Instructional Coach, I was used in a myriad of ways. Sometimes I was teaching and loving on the new teachers in the building. Other times I was used as an administrator to sit in on IEP meetings, do lunch duty, do hallway duty, do other types of 'principal-esque' things. I regularly was called in to help fix technology or teach a student or teacher how to use technology. Sometimes we flat out just did not have the subs to cover all the kids in the building, so then it became my job to cover classes. I found that Instructional Coaching was different each day as something new arose that needed my attention. I kept a few of the high flyers with me on occasion because teachers called on me to do so, and I did anything I could to serve the educators in my building. I cleaned up spills, gave bathroom breaks, covered for teachers, so they could go watch another teacher in action, completed sample lessons for teachers to see what management and innovation could look like together. If it was in my power to go help, I did. Tears were another way I helped many teachers. They would text 'SOS,' and I came running.

There was a brand new teacher I was mentoring who texted me 'help.' She was having a tough first year, huge class sizes, emergency certified, and tears were flowing on the regular. I sprinted to help her. She was fragile to say the least, both mentally, and also physically as she was pregnant and in her first trimester. A student had gotten upset with her and launched a clay coffee cup at her as hard as he could. She was hurt. Really hurt. I lept into action to help this precious teacher. She quit the very next day. Guess who covered her classes until we found a replacement? It was the instructional coach. When one of our teachers needed emergency surgery, I created her lesson plans, and checked in on her long-term sub every day. Being an 'instructional leader' has to first be about people. Being an 'instructional leader' has to be about doing what is relentlessly best for kids. We can't get to the data or lesson plans or true learning until people are seen, valued, and cared for, and the first thing you can do is serve the people.

I believe in being visible in the hallway, in the lunchroom, in classrooms, and in life. When we are visible and present, we can truly serve the people in front of us. As a leader in the school, and that is every single one of us who works in the building, we must seek out ways to serve, be seen, and see others.

See, as my good friend, Charles "Velvet Voice" Williams would say, "if serving is beneath you, leading is beyond you." As a long time educator in the public school system, I've worked at many different schools. A few years ago, our head custodian, Joe, was a person to behold. He did anything you asked. Broken Light, call Joe. Spill or worse vomit on the floor, call Joe. Any and everything Joe did and he did it well and with pride. Our school would not have run smoothly without him. I believed in his value so much that I made it my mission to serve Joe in any way I could to make his life a little bit easier. I began helping at lunch first. I wiped up spills on tables and moved the tables with Joe at all seven of our lunches. And it grew from there. I swept up messes on the floor and I always stopped by to bring Joe a treat. He was so moved by my acts, which were simple, that he came to thank me and began to weep. "I've never had a single administrator or teacher ever help me in my 25 years of being a custodian." What a shame! I wept with him.

See, friends, we are never above serving others. It is why we are here. Clean up the spill, both literally and figuratively, every day of your life and that is a life well-lived.

-Katie Kinder

Go See the Good

Taylor Upchurch

How can the school leader know the true pulse of their building from the confines of their office? It is in the classrooms where the magic happens. Principals can create plans, teams, and curriculum with the best intent. It isn't until they enter the hallways when they actually see the many cogs at work. It is the responsibility of the school leaders to create a healthy school atmosphere and ensure that students are receiving a viable curriculum. What better way to see if your plan is working than by getting up from your comfy, leather chair, behind the fancy wooden desk, and walk around your building. Leaders, get into the halls. Go see the good happening in your building.

When I need a pick-me-up or am feeling not fully present that day, I go into classrooms. My first stop, the severe and profound classroom. This is where the magic happens. I promise you will never leave that particular classroom in a worse mood than when you entered. I love talking to our students in the severe and profound room; they are our students who live with profound cognitive and physical disabilities. This is one of my favorite places to be in the whole school. I love hearing about the work they are doing or what they did in P.E. I also love to see those teachers and paraprofessionals at work. My staff members who work in this particular area of the school are pure gold. They are the best instructors in the building. They are the most patient and work through situations that many of our teachers never experience. These teachers and paraprofessionals speak to parents every day. Oftentimes, they are our school's voice to those families. Their work is vital. In addition, I wish I could insert a picture of the smile I have when I see our service learners working with our students in our special education department. It is one of my favorite things to see. I encourage you to have a conversation with your service learners and see how they are enjoying the interaction. Ask them how they have grown while working in that classroom. If for some reason you do not have student aides in your special education classes, what's holding you back? A peer mentoring program in your school can immediately foster empathy and kindness within your community. I've seen it first hand.

My second stop is a science classroom. I spent fourteen years in a science classroom, and love to hear familiar terms and see students working through experiments. When I enter a classroom, I don't go directly to the teacher and check in. I stop at desks and tables and see what students are doing. (I'm only doing this during independent work. I promise I'm not just sparking up conversations during a lecture or explanation of the assignment.) I eventually talk with the teacher and hopefully will be able to give some positive feedback. That's our goal, right, to be an instructional leader? If you're not having those conversations with kids though, you'll be missing most of the information you need to be able to provide meaningful feedback.

Many of us have lofty goals of getting into every classroom, every week or whatever your team has decided. And 90% of the time we are not able to meet that goal because "stuff" comes along. I would actually encourage you and your team to set small goals that are achievable. Remember SMART goals? I don't, sorry. But I do remember that they should be achievable, so small goals instead. My current middle school is set up by teams. There are five core teachers and three elective teachers assigned to each team. Our goal is to do an actual walkthrough with feedback to those eight teachers every other week. That's not a huge number, and hopefully we are able to create a routine that allows us to expand that number.

At some point during the day I will make my way down to the gym for a P.E. class. At forty years old, I still feel the need to show these young bucks how athletic I once was. 100% of the time I will embarrass myself and tweak a muscle in my back or roll my ankle. But I'm out there building relationships with kids. I may go one of ten from the three-point range, but there is a student there that can sink them easily and he or she wants to show you. More so than their teachers, they want to show off for the school leader. I don't know why, but it has been that way in my experience.

When I think about the words "Hallway Leadership," I think just that; be in the hallways. The hard and draining parts of our job as administrators happen behind a closed door. Assistant principals can spend hours on discipline and logging information into a computer, but I've got a big thought for you. What if being in a hallway or classroom actually would decrease the discipline problems in your school? It is your choice to stay in your office, and discipline will inevitably come to you, or you could go into the hallways and eliminate some unwanted behaviors just by being present. I'd say option two is so much more sustainable and will decrease burnout possibilities. Go see the good!

-Taylor Upchurch

CHAPTER TWENTY THREE:

Lead On, Beautiful Warriors

Katie Kinder

If you have made it this far, thank you. We've gone on the journey, and there are chapters yet to be written in your story, and in ours. We want you to tell your stories, we want to hear your stories with all the petals and the thorns encapsulated in your rose garden, in your school, in your district, in your life. We have chosen a career path in life that is never easy, but nothing worthwhile is ever simple. We lead schools, classrooms, districts, communities, and people who are fully human and messy and vulnerable and sometimes, we flat out just need one another. I hope you have found some joy, advice, hope, and comfort in these pages. Please know that we are flawed, but we continue to grow, and change, and believe in the mission of education.

This book was a labor of love for me. I'm surrounded by people I admire, look up to, learn from, and am challenged by. Many of them are highlighted in this very book, given a voice to tell the world about leadership, school, culture, and their own wisdom. If you are a new teacher, a new principal, superintendent, instructional coach, counselor, or any other type of position in which you find yourself without a support system in education, please reach out. We want to help you, keep you in this noble profession, and give you hope that there are leaders worth finding, leaders worth being, and leaders worth following out here in this wild world of education. Lead on, beautiful warriors! Our kids need you.

-Katie Kinder

FOR ADDITIONAL INFORMATION
ON OUR AUTHORS:

Katie Kinder: katie-kinder.com

Derrick Sier: derricksier.com

Taylor Upchurch: Twitter: @Taylor_Upchurch

Marcus Belin: DrMarcusBelin.com

Heady Coleman: Headycoleman.com

Shari Gateley: Twitter: @ShariGateley

Cindi Hemm: Twitter: @hemmc

Shay Omokhomion: Email: Impact2Imprint@gmail.com

Erin Patton: relatetheneducate.com

Andrea Sifers: Twitter: @SifersAndrea

Adam Welcome: mradamwelcome.com

Charles Williams: cwconsultingservice.com

Tron Young: tronyoung.com